TRAININGS in COMPASSION

MANUALS ON THE MEDITATION OF AVALOKITESHVARA

THANGTONG GYALPO • JAMGON KONGTRUL • KHAKHYAB DORJE, THE 15TH KARMAPA
CHANDRAKĪRTI • NGULCHU THOGME • THE DZOGCHEN PONLOP RINPOCHE

TRAININGS in COMPASSION

MANUALS ON THE MEDITATION OF AVALOKITESHVARA

Translated by **Tyler Dewar**
under the guidance of
The Dzogchen Ponlop Rinpoche

Commentaries by Jamgon Kongtrul and Khakhyab Dorje
Edited by Meg Miller

Snow Lion Publications
Ithaca • Boulder

Snow Lion Publications
www.SnowLionPub.com
P.O. Box 6483, Ithaca, New York 14851
tel: 607-273-8519

Printed in Canada on acid-free, recycled paper

ISBN 1-55939-206-1

This book is dedicated to Anna-Brown Griswold.

Table of Contents

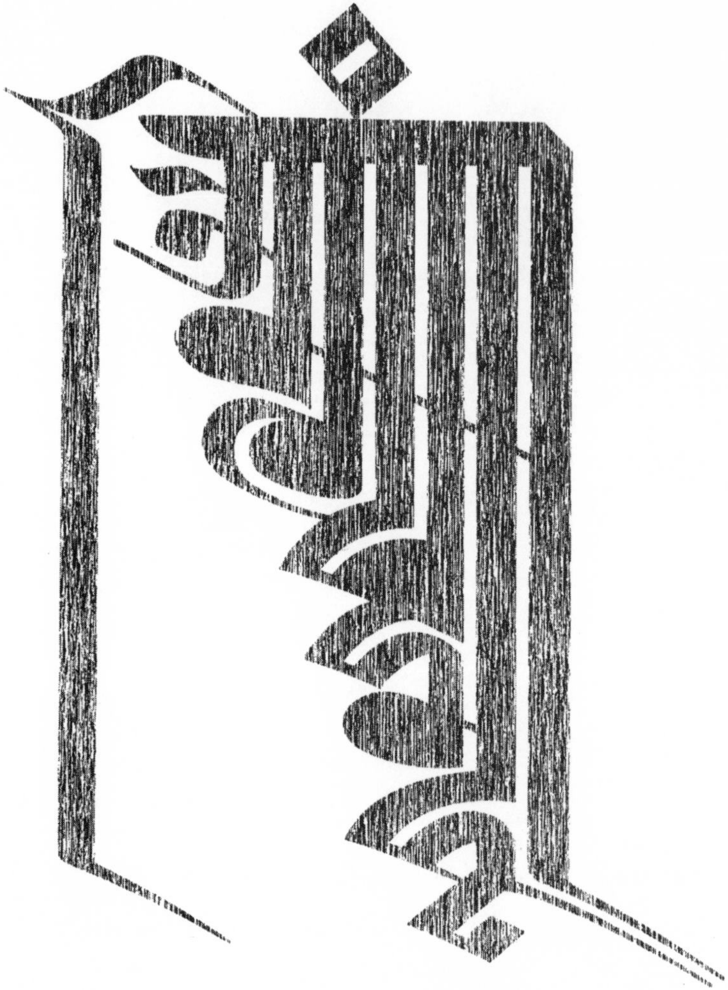

Introduction

Avalokiteshvara (Tib. *spyan ras gzigs*/"*Chenrezi*") is a bodhisattva-deity who symbolizes compassion and wisdom. Within the pantheon of deities of the Tibetan Buddhist tradition, Avalokita is considered the sovereign deity of Tibet, the "protector of the Land of Snows."

In the Mahāyāna teachings of the Buddha, Avalokita appears as a bodhisattva who participates in many dialogues with the Buddha such as the *Heart Sūtra*. In the Vajrayāna, Avalokita is a wisdom deity, or *yidam*. The yidam is a representation of the qualities of the true nature of mind with whom the meditator aligns his or her mind in order to make those qualities manifest. In particular, Avalokiteshvara is taught most frequently in connection with the qualities of loving-kindness and compassion.

THE PRESENT TRANSLATIONS

The two Kagyu commentaries on the practice of Avalokiteshvara presented in this volume are based on the famed practice liturgy or *sādhana* ("means of accomplishment") of Avalokiteshvara entitled *All-Pervading Benefit of Beings* (Tib. *'gro don mkha' khyab ma*/"*drodön kha-khyabma*"), written by the great Tibetan siddha and folk hero Thangtong Gyalpo. In addition, included here is a translation of *The Thirty-Seven Practices of Bodhisattvas* by Ngulchu Thogme, and a praise to Avalokiteshvara by the Indian master Chandrakīrti in English only. The Dzogchen Ponlop Rinpoche has graciously contributed an introductory article, *Entering the Trainings in Compassion*, to provide the reader with a context in which to encounter these vast and profound texts. For scholars and students of the Tibetan language, the original Tibetan texts of the main translated works have also been included.

The first commentary to the Avalokiteshvara sādhana, by Jamgon Kongtrul Lodrö Thaye, is written in the form of instructions to teachers who wish to confer the reading transmission for the practice of Avalokiteshvara. In this context, Kongtrul thus also provides comprehensive and practical instructions for the student. Beginning with the transmission history of the practice, Jamgon Kongtrul then guides the reader through precise stages of the approach to the practice of Avalokiteshvara. These stages may easily be broadened to apply to all dharma practice in general: reflecting on impermanence and suffering; taking refuge; engendering bodhichitta, the heartfelt wish to attain full awakening for the benefit of others; and engaging in the profound and unique method for bringing this wish to fruition—the meditation and recitation of Avalokiteshvara.

Though this text details the conferring of the reading transmission for Avalokiteshvara, it should be understood by the reader that one must have the formal authority of one's lineage masters in order to give or obtain such a reading transmission.

The second commentary was authored by the Fifteenth Gyalwa Karmapa, Khakhyab Dorje. Khakhyab Dorje beautifully adds to the points set forth by Kongtrul, guiding the practitioner word by word through the practice of Avalokiteshvara in mellifluous, poetic language. If the text of Jamgon Kongtrul has its strength in its uncompromising and penetrating exegesis of the staple elements of dharma practice, the commentary of Khakhyab Dorje excels in its instruction on the main body of deity meditation, as well as in its lucid exposition of the significance of the famed mantra OṂ MAṆI PADME HŪṂ. Next is a praise to Avalokiteshvara by the Indian master Chandrakīrti. Chandrakīrti was most renowned for his philosophical works related to to the Middle Way or *Madhyamaka*, in particular his *Entrance to the Middle Way* (Skt. *Madhyamakāvatāra*). Some readers may find very interesting the voice of lament and supplication employed by Chandrakīrti here.

Ngulchu Thogme's *The Thirty-Seven Practices of Bodhisattvas* is a cherished compendium in verse form of key instructions for training in compassion. Thogme invokes Avalokita in both the opening homage and the concluding dedication of his text, underscoring the importance of Avalokita as a symbol of compassion and altruism. *The Thirty-Seven Practices* can be chanted daily and memorized as an aid for one's practice of training in compassion.

THE AUTHORS OF THE SĀDHANA AND COMMENTARIES

Thangtong Gyalpo

The composer of the Avalokiteshvara sādhana itself, the master **Thangtong Gyalpo** (c. 1361-1485),[1] attained renown throughout Tibet for his high accomplishment as a meditator and for his contributions to Tibetan society in the fields of art and engineering. After receiving teachings from some of the greatest Tibetan masters of his time, including the great Sakya lineage master Rendawa Shönu Lodrö, Thangtong Gyalpo spent many years in solitary meditation retreat in various isolated locations in Tibet. Thereafter, envisioning benefit for the Tibetans of his time, Thangtong Gyalpo began constructing iron bridges over many of the dangerous rivers of Tibet, enabling his country's people to travel more safely than ever before. During the early phases of his bridge construction career, Thangtong Gyalpo encountered the difficulties of few laborers and poor funding. In order to overcome these difficulties, he initiated the first touring opera troupe of Tibet, consisting of his seven beautiful and talented sisters. These sisters garnered the admiration of countless Tibetans through their singing and dancing. Their performances came to be known as *lhamo*, the Tibetan word for goddess. *Lhamo* performances have continued to this day as a central pillar of Tibetan performance art.

1. Alternative dates for Thangtong Gyalpo given by some scholars are 1385-1464.

Even though Thangtong Gyalpo led an active public life, he nevertheless maintained an unwavering dedication to his spiritual life and meditation practice. This dedication is evidenced by accounts of his many sacred visions. The meditation liturgy of Avalokiteshvara is the result of one of such visions, during which Thangtong Gyalpo is said to have received the sādhana from Avalokiteshvara in person.

Jamgon Kongtrul Lodrö Thaye

Jamgon Kongtrul Lodrö Thaye (1813-1899) was a master of inconceivable qualities, foremost among the progenitors of the Ri-me or nonsectarian movement of the nineteenth century. The Ri-me movement was initiated to undermine sectarian bias prevalent in Tibet and harmful to the preservation of genuine spiritual teachings. Jamgon Kongtrul assumed great responsibilities and exerted tremendous diligence in studying and propagating the teachings of all four major Tibetan Buddhist schools. His exegetical skill is shown by the vast body of written work he left behind in the form of the renowned "five treasuries": *The Treasury of Knowledge (shes bya mdzod/"sheja dzö")*,
The Treasury of Kagyu Mantra (bka' brgyud sngags mdzod/"kagyü ngak-dzö"),
The Treasury of Precious Terma (rin chen gter mdzod/"rinchen ter-dzö"),
The Treasury of Oral Instructions (gdams ngag mdzod/"dam-ngak dzö"),
and *The Secret Treasury (gsang ba'i mdzod/"sangwe dzö")*.

These treasuries total over ninety volumes of scripture. Jamgon Kongtrul was a teacher to the famed Nyingma lineage master Ju Mipham as well as to the fourteenth and fifteenth Gyalwang Karmapas.[2]

Khakhyab Dorje

Khakhyab Dorje (1870-1921) was the fifteenth in the line of the renowned Gyalwang Karmapas, the enlightened masters who are the supreme heads of the Kagyu lineage. The lineage of Karmapas began with the first Karmapa, Düsum Khyenpa, and continues up to the present, seventeenth Karmapa, His Holiness Ogyen Trinley Dorje. Khakhyab Dorje was born in the Tsang province of central Tibet with the auspicious tuft of white hair between his eyebrows, one of the thirty-two major physical signs of a buddha. He studied with such masters as Jamgon Kongtrul Lodrö Thaye and Khenchen Tashi Özer, and he received the Kagyu lineage transmission along with the transmissions of the Five Treasuries from Kongtrul Rinpoche. Khakhyab Dorje was the first of the Gyalwang Karmapas to marry and have children. Renowned as a great master of the Terma and Dzogchen traditions, he is also venerated by many followers of the Nyingma School of Tibetan Buddhism.[3]

2. For more on the life of Jamgon Kongtrul, please see *The Autobiography of Jamgon Kongtrul: A Gem of Many Colors*, translated by Richard Barron (Ithaca: Snow Lion Publications, 2003).
3. For more on the life of Khakhyab Dorje, please see *The History of the Sixteen Karmapas of Tibet* by Karma Thinley Rinpoche (Boston: Shambhala Publications, 2001).

Acknowledgments

The translator of the texts found in this book would like extend his profound gratitude to The Dzogchen Ponlop Rinpoche, who encouraged, guided, and inspired the translations from the outset, and whose passion for the ever further transplantation of the Buddhadharma to the West continues to inspire his many students and countless others.

Sincere gratitude is also extended to the other lamas and Kagyu lineage teachers whose wisdom greatly benefited these translations: Khenpo Sonam Tobgyal Rinpoche, Lama Tashi Döndrup, and Acharya Sherab Gyaltsen Negi. The translation of *The Thirty-Seven Practices of Bodhisattvas* is based on a previous translation by Michele Martin and The Dzogchen Ponlop Rinpoche. The translation of *The Continuous Rain of Benefit to Beings*, the commentary by Khakhyab Dorje, was assisted by a previous translation by Ken McLeod. The English translation of the Avalokiteshvara sādhana was originally made by The Dzogchen Ponlop Rinpoche and the Nālandā Translation Committee and appears in revised form here. Any mistakes that remain in these works are solely those of the translator.

Thanks to Anna-Brown Griswold for her generous support of my Tibetan studies and for her friendship and example as a student. Thanks also to Scott Wellenbach of the Nālandā Translation Committee for his mentorship in translation; special gratitude to Meg Miller, who generously offered her time and editing expertise to review the manuscript of the sādhana commentaries and offer countless corrections and suggestions; to the Nalandabodhi sangha for supporting me day to day; to Nitartha Institute for providing me an opportunity to translate; to Marty and Lynne Marvet of Nitartha International for their support of the translation of the Buddhadharma; to Cindy Shelton of Nalandabodhi Publications, who oversaw the editing of the article by The Dzogchen Ponlop Rinpoche, for her continuing leadership, tirelessness, and skill in wearing many hats; to the staff of the Nitartha International Document Input Center in Kathmandu, Nepal for providing the electronic files of the Tibetan texts for the two sādhana commentaries; to Jirka Hladis for his help with Sanskrit research; to Chris Banigan for beautifying this book with his illustrations; to Steve Rhodes for his last minute editorial assistance; and finally to Sidney Piburn and all at Snow Lion Publications for their interest and support in publishing these translations.

May whatever merit there is in publishing this book be poured into the ocean of the compassionate ones' intentions, becoming a genuine cause for the swift alleviation of the suffering of beings in this and all worlds, both immediately and ultimately. May the wisdom and compassion of all beings equal that of the noble Avalokita!

Tyler Dewar
Seattle, WA
August 7, 2003

PART ONE:
Trainings in Compassion

Entering the Trainings in Compassion

The Dzogchen Ponlop Rinpoche

Entering the Trainings in Compassion

The Dzogchen Ponlop Rinpoche

When looking at the notion of enlightenment, the possibility of becoming completely awake, the only method that can lead us to that state of total wakefulness is the practice of loving-kindness and compassion.

In the sūtras, the Buddha said that in the beginning, compassion is like the seed without which we cannot have any fruit; in the middle, compassion is like water to nourish the seed we have planted; in the end, compassion is like the warmth of the sun that brings the fruit to ripening. Thus, without compassion, there is no seed of enlightenment, no path to enlightenment, and no fruition of enlightenment. The genuine heart of loving-kindness and compassion is crucial in achieving one's own freedom from suffering, and in achieving freedom for all sentient beings.

In Tibetan, the word for compassion is nying-je (Tib. *snying rje*), which literally means "noble heart." Compassion is the most dignified, noble, and profound treasure of our heart. There is nothing more profound or precious than this heart of compassion. What is this heart of compassion? It is a genuine concern, a genuine willingness to give anything of ourselves that is necessary to alleviate the sufferings of sentient beings. Compassion also has a quality of being passionate—a genuine, innocent desire and willingness, as well as a sense of openness and bravery. Bravery here refers to not being afraid of seeing and being with suffering, and to not being afraid of where you are or who you are in any given moment.

The Vast and the Profound

The path of training in the Tibetan Buddhist tradition that focuses on the development of loving-kindness and compassion is called *Mahāyāna*—the "great vehicle." All of the many Mahāyāna teachings are included within two categories: the vast and the profound. These two qualities correlate to the two types of bodhichitta, absolute bodhichitta and relative bodhichitta. Absolute bodhichitta is the profound reality, and relative bodhichitta is the vast methods for connecting to that reality.

Relative Bodhichitta: The Gateway to Absolute Truth

In order to genuinely connect with the profound reality of absolute bodhichitta, we must approach it through the vast methods of relative bodhichitta. Although the profound nature of reality may seem easy to theorize, it is actually very difficult to experience in a nonconceptual and immediate way. To work towards this nonconceptual understanding of the absolute truth, we need the path and practices of relative bodhichitta. Without such a path, our profound theories may sound nice, but they will still not have any true effect on our mindstream. In order to make manifest the profound nature of reality in our hearts and in our world, we need the vast methods of relative bodhichitta, the trainings in compassion.

Training in compassion has the capacity to be both profound and vast—both absolute and relative. Compassion has the quality of being approachable and at the same time ungraspable. It manifests both the quality of shūnyatā, emptiness, or egolessness, as well as the qualities of kindness and joyfulness. Therefore, from the Mahāyāna point of view, compassion is the most important practice we could ever engage in. It can lead us to the full realization of enlightenment without any need for other practices.

Our Own Pain: The First Training in Compassion

Compassion must start with seeing our own suffering. If it does not, then seeing the suffering of others will be merely conceptual. It will merely be a matter of having learned about suffering from a book or philosophy. We may intellectually know about the different types of suffering and so forth, but without inward reflection, our understanding will always be a theoretical knowledge that is directed toward the outside. Starting from our own experience of suffering becomes most important for the practice of open and genuine compassion.

Being present with the immediate experience of our own suffering is, from a certain perspective, a great spiritual practice. Yet from another perspective, we have no choice but to be accompanied by our suffering. Therefore, why not use our suffering in a positive way, instead of wasting our time? Our usual reaction to suffering is to want to be somewhere else or someone else as soon as it arises. If such wishing actually improved our suffering, then perhaps there would be an argument for staying with that approach. Yet, as we know, regardless of what escape routes we create, we will still be stuck with our headaches, our painful emotions, and our irritations.

The most effective and powerful way to deal with suffering and unpleasant circumstances is to be within those very states without any hesitation, without any kind of fear.

Fear and Fearlessness

Perhaps the first reaction we have to our own suffering is fear. Fear arises in us almost automatically when we experience strong emotions or pain. We don't have to sit there and generate fear—it just arises. When we experience a disturbing emotion such as jealousy we think, "No, I don't want this." We would rather not experience it. However, if we examine fear closely, we see that it is a thought to which we have been habituating our mind for a very long time. We have repeated this thought pattern of fear for many years, and from a Buddhist point of view, many lifetimes.

In just the same way, when we habituate our minds to being fearless, to being brave and open towards our emotions, fearlessness will also arise naturally. In order for this to happen we must train in applying antidotes to our thought patterns that are caught up in fear. In this way, we transcend fear first through a conceptual process, which later becomes nonconceptual, a natural fearlessness. In order to become fearless in this way, we need determination and the willingness to face our emotions. With that strong determination and courage, fearlessness will arise effortlessly.

Compassion and Egolessness

Compassion, this genuine heartfelt concern for others, arises on the basis of a certain degree of understanding egolessness. When you give love to someone without any ego or self-interest, that love and concern is genuine compassion, the "noble heart." As long as we have a strong ego, our practice of compassion will still be slightly selfish and not very genuine. Such compassion involves an uncertain motivation, a motivation that mixes the interests of other beings with our own self-interest. Therefore, in order to make our compassion more genuine, we need to also be familiar with the understanding of egolessness—selflessness—the absolute nature of compassion. The most genuine and absolute nature of compassion is completely free of any ego.

Checking Our Motivation

When we extend compassion, it is important for us to reflect on what our motivations are. What is our heart saying when we are trying to take on the suffering of others, when we are trying to give others happiness? Sometimes we do things that may look like compassionate acts, but in fact they are actually more selfish than compassionate. For example, when we have a pet dog or cat and they are sick or dying, we feel terrible. We feel sad and full of compassion towards that being. When they are gone, we shed tears for many days and experience the pain of losing them. Yet when we examine our hearts, are we really shedding these tears with genuine concern for the interests of that being? Or are we shedding these tears because we miss their companionship? If it is the former, then our compassion is genuine. However, if it is the latter, then that is a self-centered motivation. Our main motivation is not compassion for our pet, but rather our own desire not to be alone after losing their companionship. Starting from such examinations, we can check our attitude continually and see how genuine the compassion is that we are trying to make manifest.

The Three Types of Compassion

Compassion that Focuses on Sentient Beings

There are three elements of compassion. The first is compassion that focuses on sentient beings. In this type of compassion, there is a sense of duality, a split between subject and object. The object is all sentient beings and the subject is the noble heart of compassion. We try to extend this noble heart without any boundaries.

This practice of compassion begins at home. We have our parents, our children, and our brothers and sisters, who perhaps irritate us the most, and we begin our practice of loving-kindness and compassion with them. Then gradually we extend our compassion out into our greater community, our country, neighbouring countries, the world, and finally to all sentient beings equally without exception.

Extending compassion in this way makes it evident that it is not very easy to instantly have compassion for "all sentient beings." Theoretically it may be comfortable to have compassion for "all sentient beings," but through our practice we realize that "all sentient beings" is a collection of individuals. When we actually try to generate compassion for each and every individual, it becomes much more challenging. But if we cannot work with one individual, then how can we work with all sentient beings? Therefore it is important for us to reflect more practically, to work with compassion for individuals and then extend that compassion further.

There are two ways to begin practicing this first type of compassion. We could begin with someone close to us, or we could begin from the other extreme, with someone who is neutral. Whichever approach we choose, our compassion must reach the same level in the end, which is equal and unbiased compassion for all beings. At some point, we have to reach a level where we feel, "It doesn't matter if they irritate me, or whether they love me or hate me, I want to practice compassion."

In this context, we can cultivate compassion even for those who have harmed us or those who have harmed our loved ones. When people cause harm to other beings, they are doing so because they themselves are suffering, even though sometimes they may appear to be enjoying their aggression. If we go further into their heart and explore their experience more, we can see that they are experiencing great pain.

Working first in this way with loving-kindness and compassion involving the conceptual distinctions of subject and object is thus an approachable practice. It is not something too abstract or absolute.

Compassion Focusing on the Nature of Phenomena

The second aspect of compassion is called *compassion focusing on the nature of phenomena*. This type of compassion is much deeper. Here we are not just looking at someone's obvious suffering. We are looking at their basic confusion and cultivating the genuine wish for them to possess great wisdom, compassion, and love. When we practice compassion, instead of concentrating only on the faults of others we begin to see that the faults of these beings arise from their confusion and ignorance.

Thus, not only do we want them to be free from their temporary sufferings of body and mind, we also want them to be rich in wisdom and compassion. We see how beings are suffering from a lack of wisdom and compassion and want them to enjoy such genuine causes of happiness.

Non-Referential Compassion

The third type of compassion is *non-referential compassion*, which comprises the absolute aspect of compassion. At some point after we have become familiar with the first two types of compassion, we begin to feel natural love when we see sentient beings. This love is an unconditional desire to experience the ultimate reality. It arises spontaneously, without concept. There are no thoughts saying, "I want him to be free from suffering," or "I want her to have wisdom." There is simply a non-conceptual experience of compassion that arises as soon as one sees sentient beings. This type of compassion is synonymous with the realization of egolessness, selflessness, and emptiness.

An example we can give for this third type of compassion is that of a mother's love for her only child. This example is not the same as the actual non-referential compassion, but it is the only example that comes close to illustrating its qualities. In the example, a mother has only one child, from whom she has been separated for a long time. When she sees her child again, the child is going through extreme pain. For the mother, that first glimpse of the child contains nothing but love. A genuine compassion arises beyond words and concepts. There is only a vivid feeling. Like that, the Buddha and bodhisattvas experience compassion for all sentient beings.

The View of Training in Compassion

How do we train our mind in love and compassion? We train our mind by viewing our basic life situation as a totally positive environment for us to extend out and manifest our noble heart of enlightenment. We see that there is a possibility for us to make friends with what we usually see as unfavorable. We can make friends with the things that we usually reject, that we run away from in our ordinary lives. At the same time, through these mind trainings we also learn how to open our hearts and give our greatest gift, which is compassion, love, and kindness. Not only do we give spiritual wisdom, we also give whatever feels most precious in our heart in everyday life.

Through these mind trainings we are learning how to make our heart soft and at the same time strong and compassionate. Being compassionate does not mean just being totally vulnerable and open and giving everything we have away. There is a sense of taking our own ground, our own seat of wisdom. Through this we come to have discernment about what is most needed in any given situation.

The Preliminaries for Training in Compassion: The Four Reminders and Guru Yoga

The practice of training in compassion begins with the preliminary practices. The training in the preliminaries involves two aspects. The first is reflecting on the "four reminders," the four thoughts that turn the mind away from saṃsāra. The second is the practice of guru yoga.

The Four Reminders

The four reminders are the reflections on the precious human birth, death and impermanence, karmic cause and effect, and the shortcomings of saṃsāra.

Precious Human Birth

When we reflect on the preciousness of our human birth, we are developing an appreciation for every moment. This moment, when we can sit and generate bodhichitta, is precious. This moment of being aware and mindful is precious. And this moment of being free from severe pain and suffering, both physically and mentally, is also precious. Of course, we all feel that we have a lot of suffering, but if we reflect carefully, we can see how that evaluation is very relative. When we turn on our television or read the news, we see that our pain is minimal in comparison to the pain of the rest of the world, pain such as hunger, famine, warfare, and so on.

We have this moment to sit and practice, to reflect on our suffering and the suffering of others, and to reflect on bringing enlightenment into the hearts of all sentient beings. Actually, every experience that we go through in twenty-four hours is a very profound experience. This first reflection involves being where we are, and appreciating who we are. We even appreciate all the emotions and ego-clinging that arise.

Precious human birth also involves working with self-hatred. Self-hatred arises out of not appreciating the moment, not appreciating who we are and where we are. There is a sense of a sharp edge that we are turning against ourselves, and this is causing a lot of unnecessary pain. So from a Mahāyāna point of view, we begin reflecting on the preciousness of this moment—wherever we are, whatever we are experiencing. There is a profound reality there, and a great moment of opportunity and hope. Hope for what? The hope of awakening ourselves and others in this very moment.

Death and Impermanence

Once we have appreciated this precious moment of our human birth, we then reflect upon death and impermanence and see that this moment is not permanent: this existence is not going to be here forever. This reality of our precious existence is not frozen. It is like a flowing river—every moment is new. If we do not take full advantage of this very moment, it's going to slip away from our hands like it has in the past. That is what we call impermanence. If we are not taking full advantage of our chance to be awake, to be free, to appreciate, then this moment is going to slip away from our hands. It's not going to remain. If we waive this opportunity, then we don't know when it will arise again. We may go to bed fine, but when we wake up we may be in the hospital.

We should see this transitory nature of our lives, the fragile nature of our existence. It is so fragile that we cannot afford to drop it. We need to hold it with great mindfulness and care. This is the reflection on impermanence: seeing how fragile our life is, how fragile this moment is, and how easily we can lose this opportunity. That reality of impermanence helps us to appreciate our precious human life. In this way, the contemplations of impermanence and precious human birth go hand-in-hand. Contemplating these two together in itself becomes a very powerful preliminary practice.

Karmic Cause and Effect

The third contemplation is that of karma, cause and effect. Karma refers to the actions we take in this moment, and to how those actions have consequences. This third reflection deals with how to make the best use of this precious and fleeting moment, our human life. Having first seen the preciousness and impermanence of our lives, we then focus on how we relate to this moment in our actions, trying to pay attention to how we can act as appropriately as we can. This involves developing the wisdom and courage to do beneficial things for ourselves and others.

The Shortcomings of Saṃsāra

The fourth reflection is that of the shortcomings of saṃsāra. In some ways this is a rather straightforward contemplation. In every moment, we find plenty of things to complain about. The shortcomings of saṃsāra basically refers to the three sufferings: all-pervasive suffering, the suffering of change, and the suffering of suffering. From the Buddhist point of view, every moment of saṃsāra entails these three sufferings.

All-pervasive suffering is the most basic form of suffering, the suffering of impermanence. Whatever type of moment we are involved in, we have no power to stay another moment in that same state. We must move on. There is no way to extend that moment, nor is there a way for us to skip that moment and go to the next. Such reality of impermanence is all-pervasive. Another way of defining all-pervasive suffering is basic fear. It is the fear that we experience of losing something dear to our heart, or of meeting with something that is undesirable. This basic fear is an underlying factor of every moment of saṃsāra. In every moment, we have this fear related to losing something we want or meeting with something we do not want.

This form of suffering also involves our basic habitual pattern of having little contentment. For example, I rarely meet people who say to me, "I am happy with my job." There is always something to complain about. Similarly, no matter how much wealth or enjoyments we have, still we cannot find satisfaction. This all-pervasive suffering is the most difficult of the three sufferings to recognize in our day-to-day lives. The other two sufferings, the suffering of change and the suffering of suffering, are easier to understand. In brief, the fourth reminder, the shortcomings of saṃsāra, is the reflection on the suffering and dissatisfaction of saṃsāric existence.

Guru Yoga

The second stage of the preliminary practices is to connect with the principle of enlightened masters through the practice of guru yoga.

It is not sufficient for us to simply reflect on these four reminders and try to practice the trainings in compassion on our own. We must also connect with some encouragement from the enlightened hearts of the masters who have perfected these practices. This could mean connecting to enlightened masters of the past, or connecting to enlightened masters of the present and future.

Avalokiteshvara

For example, we can reflect on the realization and compassion of Avalokiteshvara. With a heart of appreciation for his wisdom and compassion, we make a connection to the reality of our own enlightened heart. That same heart of enlightenment of Avalokiteshvara is right here within ourselves. If we can appreciate the enlightened masters in this way, it becomes a powerful experience in our everyday lives.

As a method for engendering such appreciation, we traditionally either visualize an enlightened master in the space in front of us, or we visualize him or her above the crown of our heads. We can visualize or look at a picture of Avalokiteshvara, thinking about him, and thinking about his blessings of wisdom and compassion. We invoke his blessing and presence and, at the end of the visualization, imagine that he dissolves into us and becomes inseparable from us. This is a method of connecting with our own heart of buddha nature. Whatever appears outside is actually a reflection of our own heart of enlightenment. This heart is our primary state of being. When we become one with Avalokiteshvara, or any another master, we invoke and connect with the heart of enlightenment. Thus the blessing that we receive in this practice is the blessing of our own buddha nature.

When we do the practice of Avalokiteshvara, we are generating the heart of compassion, trying to live with this heart, trying to manifest this heart in everyday life as well as in our spiritual practice. It becomes very important for Mahāyāna practice.

In sum, the preliminaries for training in compassion are the reflections on the four reminders, followed by some kind of guru yoga. If we choose to meditate on Avalokiteshvara as our guru yoga practice, we can also recite his six-syllable mantra, Oṃ Maṇi Padme Hūṃ.

The Dzogchen Ponlop Rinpoche is acknowledged as one of the foremost scholars and educators of his generation in the Nyingma and Kagyu Schools of Tibetan Buddhism. Rinpoche founded and continues to direct the activities of Nitartha *international*, Nalandabodhi, and Nitartha Institute, which focus on the preservation of endangered ancient texts, study and meditation training, and traditional Buddhist education. An accomplished meditation master, calligrapher, visual artist and poet, Rinpoche is also fluent in the English language and known for his sharp intellect, humor, and the lucidity of his teaching style. Well-versed in Western culture and technology, he is the primary architect for the many websites under the Nalandabodhi umbrella and publisher of **Bodhi Magazine**, an internationally distributed periodical. More information on Rinpoche and his activities can be found at **www.nalandabodhi.org** and **www.nitartha.org.**

༄༅།། ཐུགས་རྗེ་ཆེན་པོའི་བསྒོམ་བཟླས་འགྲོ་དོན་མཁའ་ཁྱབ་མ་བཞུགས་སོ།

All-Pervading Benefit of Beings

The Meditation and Recitation of the Great Compassionate One

by Thangtong Gyalpo

༄༅། །ཐུགས་རྗེ་ཆེན་པོའི་བསྒོམ་བཟླས་འགྲོ་དོན་མཁའ་ཁྱབ་མ་བཞུགས་སོ།

All-Pervading Benefit of Beings

The Meditation and Recitation of the Great Compassionate One

སྐྱབས་འགྲོ་སེམས་བསྐྱེད་ནི།

REFUGE AND BODHICHITTA:

སངས་རྒྱས་ཆོས་དང་ཚོགས་ཀྱི་མཆོག་རྣམས་ལ།

SANG GYE CHÖ DANG TSHOK KYI CHOK NAM LA

In the supreme Buddha, dharma, and assembly,

བྱང་ཆུབ་བར་དུ་བདག་ནི་སྐྱབས་སུ་མཆི།

CHANG CHUB BAR DU DAK NI KYAP SU CHI

I take refuge until attaining enlightenment.

བདག་གིས་སྦྱིན་སོགས་བགྱིས་པའི་བསོད་ནམས་ཀྱིས།

DAK GI JIN SOK GYI PE SÖ NAM KYI

Through the merit of practicing generosity and so on,

འགྲོ་ལ་ཕན་ཕྱིར་སངས་རྒྱས་འགྲུབ་པར་ཤོག །

DRO LA PHEN CHIR SANG GYE DRUP PAR SHOK

May I attain buddhahood in order to benefit beings.

ལན་གསུམ།

Repeat three times.

ལྷ་བསྐྱེད་ནི།

VISUALIZING THE DEITY:

བདག་སོགས་མཁའ་ཁྱབ་སེམས་ཅན་གྱི།

DAK SOK KHA KHYAB SEM CEN GYI

On the crown of my head and those of others,
sentient beings pervading space,

སྤྱི་གཙུག་པད་དཀར་ཟླ་བའི་སྟེང་།

CI TSUK PE KAR DA WE TENG

On a white lotus and moon,

ཧྲཱིཿལས་འཕགས་མཆོག་སྤྱན་རས་གཟིགས།
HRI LE PHAK CHOK CEN RE ZI
From HRĪḤ, appears noble and supreme Avalokita.

དཀར་གསལ་འོད་ཟེར་ལྔ་ལྡན་འཕྲོ།
KAR SAL Ö ZER NGA DEN THRO
He is brilliant white and radiates the five lights.

མཛེས་འཛུམ་ཐུགས་རྗེའི་སྤྱན་གྱིས་གཟིགས།
DZE DZUM THUK JEY CEN GYI ZIK
Handsome and smiling, he looks on with eyes
of compassion.

ཕྱག་བཞིའི་དང་པོ་ཐལ་སྦྱར་མཛད།
CHAK ZHI DANG PO THAL JAR DZE
He has four hands: the first are joined in añjali;

འོག་གཉིས་ཤེལ་ཕྲེང་པད་དཀར་བསྣམས།
OK NYI SHEL THRENG PE KAR NAM
The lower two hold a crystal māla and a white lotus.

དར་དང་རིན་ཆེན་རྒྱན་གྱིས་སྤྲས།
DAR DANG RIN CHEN GYEN GYI TRE
Adorned with ornaments of silks and jewels,

རི་དྭགས་པགས་པས་སྟོད་གཡོག་གསོལ།
RI DAK PAK PE TÖ YOK SÖL
He wears an upper garment of deerskin.

འོད་དཔག་མེད་པའི་དབུ་རྒྱན་ཅན།
Ö PAK ME PE U GYEN CEN
Amitābha crowns his head.

ཞབས་གཉིས་རྡོ་རྗེ་སྐྱིལ་ཀྲུང་བཞུགས།
ZHAP NYI DOR JE KYIL TRUNG ZHUK
His two feet are in the vajra posture.

དྲི་མེད་ཟླ་བར་རྒྱབ་བརྟེན་པ།
DRI ME DA WAR GYAP TEN PA
His back rests against a stainless moon.

སྐྱབས་གནས་ཀུན་འདུས་ངོ་བོར་གྱུར།
KYAP NE KÜN DÜ NGO WOR GYUR
He is the embodiment of all objects of refuge.

བདག་དང་སེམས་ཅན་ཐམས་ཅད་ཀྱིས་མགྲིན་གཅིག་ཏུ་གསོལ་བ་འདེབས་པར་བསམ་ལ།
Think that you and all sentient beings are supplicating with one voice:

ཇོ་བོ་སྐྱོན་གྱིས་མ་གོས་སྐུ་མདོག་དཀར།
JO WO KYÖN GYI MA GÖ KU DOK KAR
Lord, white in color, unstained by faults,

རྫོགས་སངས་རྒྱས་ཀྱིས་དབུ་ལ་བརྒྱན།
DZOK SANG GYE KYI U LA GYEN
A perfect buddha adorning your head,

ཐུགས་རྗེའི་སྤྱན་གྱིས་འགྲོ་ལ་གཟིགས།
THUK JEY CEN GYI DRO LA ZIK
You look upon beings with eyes of compassion.

སྤྱན་རས་གཟིགས་ལ་ཕྱག་འཚལ་ལོ།
CEN RE ZI LA CHAK TSHAL LO
Avalokita, we prostrate to you.

ཞེས་ཅི་ནུས་བསགས།
Recite that as many times as you can.

ཡན་ལག་བདུན་པ་ནི།
THE SEVEN-BRANCH PRAYER:

འཕགས་མཆོག་སྤྱན་རས་གཟིགས་དབང་དང་།
PHAK CHOK CEN RE ZI WANG DANG
To noble lord Avalokita

ཕྱོགས་བཅུ་དུས་གསུམ་བཞུགས་པ་ཡི།
CHOK CU DÜ SUM ZHUK PA YI
And to all the buddhas and their heirs

རྒྱལ་བ་སྲས་བཅས་ཐམས་ཅད་ལ།
GYAL WA SE CE THAM CE LA
Of the ten directions and three times,

ཀུན་ནས་དང་བས་ཕྱག་འཚལ་ལོ།
KÜN NE DANG WE CHAK TSHAL LO
We prostrate with lucid faith.

མེ་ཏོག་སྡུག་སྤོས་མར་མེ་དྲི།

ME TOK DUK PÖ MAR ME DRI

We make offerings, those actual and those emanated by mind:

ཞལ་ཟས་རོལ་མོ་ལ་སོགས་པ།

ZHAL ZE RÖL MO LA SOK PA

Flowers, incense, light, perfume,

དངོས་འབྱོར་ཡིད་ཀྱིས་སྤྲུལ་ནས་ཕུལ།

NGÖ JOR YI KYI TRÜL NE PHÜL

Food, music, and so on.

འཕགས་པའི་ཚོགས་ཀྱིས་བཞེས་སུ་གསོལ།

PHAK PE TSHOK KYI ZHE SU SOL

Assembly of noble ones, please accept them.

ཐོག་མ་མེད་ནས་ད་ལྟའི་བར།

THOK MA ME NE DA TE BAR

We confess all the negative actions

མི་དགེ་བཅུ་དང་མཚམས་མེད་ལྔ།

MI GE CU DANG TSHAM ME NGA

We have committed from beginningless time until now,

སེམས་ནི་ཉོན་མོངས་དབང་གྱུར་པའི།

SEM NI NYÖN MONG WANG GYUR PE

Due to our minds being overpowered
by the mental afflictions:

སྡིག་པ་ཐམས་ཅད་བཤགས་པར་བགྱི།

DIK PA THAM CE SHAK PAR GYI

The ten nonvirtuous actions and the five acts
of immediate consequence.

ཉན་ཐོས་རང་རྒྱལ་བྱང་ཆུབ་སེམས།

NYEN THÖ RANG GYAL CHANG CHUB SEM

We rejoice in the merit

སོ་སོའི་སྐྱེ་བོ་ལ་སོགས་པས།

SO SÖ KYE WO LA SOK PE

Of whatever virtue has been accumulated

དུས་གསུམ་དགེ་བ་ཅི་བསགས་པའི།

DÜ SUM GE WA CI SAK PE

By hearers, solitary realizers, bodhisattvas,

བསོད་ནམས་ལ་ནི་བདག་ཡི་རང་།

SÖ NAM LA NI DAK YI RANG

And ordinary beings throughout the three times.

སེམས་ཅན་རྣམས་ཀྱི་བསམ་པ་དང་།

SEM CEN NAM KYI SAM PA DANG

In accordance with the diverse capabilities

བློ་ཡི་བྱེ་བྲག་ཇི་ལྟ་བར།

LO YI JE DRAK JI TA WAR

And aspirations of sentient beings,

ཆེ་ཆུང་ཐུན་མོང་ཐེག་པ་ཡི།

CHE CHUNG THUN MONG THEK PA YI

We request you to turn the wheel of dharma

ཆོས་ཀྱི་འཁོར་ལོ་བསྐོར་དུ་གསོལ།

CHÖ KYI KHOR LO KOR DU SÖL

Of the greater, lesser, or conventional vehicles.

འཁོར་བ་ཇི་སྲིད་མ་སྟོངས་བར།

KHOR WA JI SI MA TONG BAR

Not passing into nirvāṇa

མྱ་ངན་མི་འདའ་ཐུགས་རྗེ་ཡིས།

NYA NGEN MI DA THUK JE YI

Until saṃsāra is emptied,

སྡུག་བསྔལ་རྒྱ་མཚོར་བྱིང་བ་ཡི།

DUK NGEL GYAM TSHOR JING WA YI

Please look with compassion on sentient beings

སེམས་ཅན་རྣམས་ལ་གཟིགས་སུ་གསོལ།

SEM CAN NAM LA ZIK SU SÖL

Drowning in the ocean of suffering.

བདག་གིས་བསོད་ནམས་ཅི་བསགས་པ།

DAK GI SÖ NAM CI SAK PA
May whatever merit we have accumulated

ཐམས་ཅད་བྱང་ཆུབ་རྒྱུར་གྱུར་ནས།

THAM CE CHANG CHUB GYUR GYUR NE
Become a cause for enlightenment.

རིང་པོར་མི་ཐོགས་འགྲོ་བ་ཡི།

RING POR MI THOK DRO WA YI
Without delay, may we become

འདྲེན་པའི་དཔལ་དུ་བདག་གྱུར་ཅིག །

DREN PE PAL DU DAK GYUR CIK
A glorious guide for beings.

གདུང་འབོད་ཀྱི་གསོལ་འདེབས་ནི།

THE SUPPLICATION OF CALLING WITH LONGING:

གསོལ་བ་འདེབས་སོ་བླ་མ་སྤྱན་རས་གཟིགས།

SÖL WA DEP SO LA MA CEN RE ZI
We supplicate you, guru Avalokita.

གསོལ་བ་འདེབས་སོ་ཡི་དམ་སྤྱན་རས་གཟིགས།

SÖL WA DEP SO YI DAM CEN RE ZI
We supplicate you, yidam Avalokita.

གསོལ་བ་འདེབས་སོ་འཕགས་མཆོག་སྤྱན་རས་གཟིགས།

SÖL WA DEP SO PHAK CHOK CEN RE ZI
We supplicate you, supreme noble Avalokita.

གསོལ་བ་འདེབས་སོ་སྐྱབས་མགོན་སྤྱན་རས་གཟིགས།

SÖL WA DEP SO KYAP GÖN CEN RE ZI
We supplicate you, lord of refuge Avalokita.

གསོལ་བ་འདེབས་སོ་བྱམས་མགོན་སྤྱན་རས་གཟིགས།

SÖL WA DEP SO CHAM GÖN CEN RE ZI
We supplicate you, loving protector Avalokita.

ཐུགས་རྗེས་ཟུངས་ཤིག་རྒྱལ་བ་ཐུགས་རྗེ་ཅན།

THUK JE ZUNG SHIK GYAL WA THUK JE CEN

Hold us in your compassion, compassionate victorious one.

མཐའ་མེད་འཁོར་བར་གྲངས་མེད་འཁྱམས་གྱུར་ཅིང་།

THA ME KHOR WAR DRANG ME KHYAM GYUR CING

For beings who have wandered through countless aeons
in endless saṃsāra

བཟོད་མེད་སྡུག་བསྔལ་མྱོང་བའི་འགྲོ་བ་ལ།

ZÖ ME DUK NGEL NYONG WE DRO WA LA

And experience unbearable suffering,

མགོན་པོ་ཁྱེད་ལས་སྐྱབས་གཞན་མ་མཆིས་སོ།

GÖN PO KHYE LE KYAP ZHEN MA CHI SO

There is no other refuge but you, lord.

རྣམ་མཁྱེན་སངས་རྒྱས་ཐོབ་པར་བྱིན་གྱིས་རློབས།

NAM KHYEN SANG GYE THOP PAR JIN GYI LOP

Grant your blessing that they may achieve
omniscient buddhahood.

ཐོག་མེད་དུས་ནས་ལས་ངན་བསགས་པའི་མཐུས།

THOK ME DÜ NE LE NGEN SAK PE THÜ

Accumulating negative karma from
beginningless time,

ཞེ་སྡང་དབང་གིས་དམྱལ་བར་སྐྱེས་གྱུར་ཏེ།

ZHE DANG WANG GI NYAL WAR KYE GYUR TE

Due to aggression, sentient beings are born
in the hells

ཚ་གྲང་སྡུག་བསྔལ་མྱོང་བའི་སེམས་ཅན་རྣམས།

TSHA DRANG DUK NGEL NYONG WE SEM CEN NAM

And experience the sufferings of hot and cold.

ལྷ་མཆོག་ཁྱེད་ཀྱི་དྲུང་དུ་སྐྱེ་བར་ཤོག །

LHA CHOK KHYE KYI DRUNG DU KYE WAR SHOK

May they be born in your presence, supreme deity.

ཨོཾ་མ་ཎི་པདྨེ་ཧཱུྃ།

OM MANI PEME HUNG

OṂ MAṆI PADME HŪṂ

ཐོག་མེད་དུས་ནས་ལས་ངན་བསགས་པའི་མཐུས།
THOK ME DÜ NE LE NGEN SAK PE THÜ
Accumulating negative karma from beginningless time,

སེར་སྣའི་དབང་གིས་ཡི་དྭགས་གནས་སུ་སྐྱེས།
SER NE WANG GI YI DAK NE SU KYE
Due to miserliness, sentient beings are born in the hungry ghost realm

བཀྲེས་སྐོམ་སྡུག་བསྔལ་མྱོང་བའི་སེམས་ཅན་རྣམས།
TRE KOM DUK NGEL NYONG WE SEM CEN NAM
And experience the sufferings of hunger and thirst.

ཞིང་མཆོག་པོ་ཏ་ལ་རུ་སྐྱེ་བར་ཤོག །
ZHING CHOK PO TA LA RU KYE WAR SHOK
May they be born in your supreme pure land of Potala.

ཨོཾ་མ་ཎི་པདྨེ་ཧཱུྃ།
OM MANI PEME HUNG
OṂ MAṆI PADME HŪṂ

ཐོག་མེད་དུས་ནས་ལས་ངན་བསགས་པའི་མཐུས།
THOK ME DÜ NE LE NGEN SAK PE THÜ
Accumulating negative karma from beginningless time,

གཏི་མུག་དབང་གིས་དུད་འགྲོར་སྐྱེས་གྱུར་ཏེ།
TI MUK WANG GI DÜ DROR KYE GYUR TE
Due to bewilderment, sentient beings are born as animals

གླེན་ལྐུག་སྡུག་བསྔལ་མྱོང་བའི་སེམས་ཅན་རྣམས།
LEN KUK DUG NGEL NYONG WE SEM CEN NAM
And experience the sufferings of stupidity and dullness.

མགོན་པོ་ཁྱེད་ཀྱི་དྲུང་དུ་སྐྱེ་བར་ཤོག
GÖN PO KHYE KYI DRUNG DU KYE WAR SHOK
May they be born in your presence, protector.

ཨོཾ་མ་ཎི་པདྨེ་ཧཱུྃ།
OM MANI PEME HUNG
OṂ MAṆI PADME HŪṂ

ཐོག་མེད་དུས་ནས་ལས་ངན་བསགས་པའི་མཐུས།
THOK ME DÜ NE LE NGEN SAK PE THÜ
Accumulating negative karma from beginningless time,

འདོད་ཆགས་དབང་གིས་མི་ཡི་གནས་སུ་སྐྱེས།
DÖ CHAK WANG GI MI YI NE SU KYE
Due to desire, sentient beings are born
in the human realm

བྲེལ་ཕོངས་སྡུག་བསྔལ་མྱོང་བའི་སེམས་ཅན་རྣམས།
DREL PHONG DUK NGEL NYONG WE SEM CEN NAM
And experience the sufferings of constant toil
and poverty.

ཞིང་མཆོག་བདེ་བ་ཅན་དུ་སྐྱེ་བར་ཤོག །
ZHING CHOK DE WA CEN KYE WAR SHOK
May they be born in your pure land of Sukhāvatī.

ཨོཾ་མ་ཎི་པདྨེ་ཧཱུྃ།
OM MANI PEME HUNG
OṂ MAṆI PADME HŪṂ

ཐོག་མེད་དུས་ནས་ལས་ངན་བསགས་པའི་མཐུས།
THOK ME DÜ NE LE NGEN SAK PE THÜ
Accumulating negative karma from beginningless time,

ཕྲག་དོག་དབང་གིས་ལྷ་མིན་གནས་སུ་སྐྱེས།
THRAK DOK WANG GI LHA MIN NE SU KYE
Due to jealousy, sentient beings are born in the realm
of the jealous gods

འཐབ་རྩོད་སྡུག་བསྔལ་མྱོང་བའི་སེམས་ཅན་རྣམས།
THAP TSÖ DUK NGEL NYONG WE SEM CEN NAM
And experience the sufferings of constant fighting
and quarreling.

པོ་ཏ་ལ་ཡི་ཞིང་དུ་སྐྱེ་བར་ཤོག
PO TA LA YI ZHING DU KYE WAR SHOK
May they be born in your pure land of Potala.

ཨོཾ་མ་ཎི་པདྨེ་ཧཱུྃ།
OM MANI PEME HUNG
OṂ MAṆI PADME HŪṂ

ཐོག་མེད་དུས་ནས་ལས་ངན་བསགས་པའི་མཐུས།
THOG ME DÜ NE LE NGEN SAK PE THÜ
Accumulating negative karma from
beginningless time,

ང་རྒྱལ་དབང་གིས་ལྷ་ཡི་གནས་སུ་སྐྱེས།
NGA GYAL WANG GI LHA YI NE SU KYE
Due to pride, sentient beings are born
in the realm of the gods

འཕོ་ལྟུང་སྡུག་བསྔལ་མྱོང་བའི་སེམས་ཅན་རྣམས།
PHO TUNG DUK NGEL NYONG WE SEM CEN NAM
And experience the sufferings of death and falling.

པོ་ཏ་ལ་ཡི་ཞིང་དུ་སྐྱེ་བར་ཤོག
PO TA LA YI ZHING DU KYE WAR SHOK
May they be born in your land of Potala.

ཨོཾ་མ་ཎི་པདྨེ་ཧཱུྃ།
OM MANI PEME HUNG
OṂ MAṆI PADME HŪṂ

བདག་ནི་སྐྱེ་ཞིང་སྐྱེ་བ་ཐམས་ཅད་དུ།
DAK NI KYE ZHING KYE WA THAM CE DU
Birth after birth, through all our lives,

སྤྱན་རས་གཟིགས་དང་མཛད་པ་མཚུངས་པ་ཡིས།
CEN RE ZI DANG DZE PA TSHUNG PA YI
May we liberate beings of the impure realms

མ་དག་ཞིང་གི་འགྲོ་རྣམས་སྒྲོལ་བ་དང་།
MA DAK ZHING GI DRO NAM DRÖL WA DANG
By activity equal to yours, Avalokita,

གསུང་མཆོག་ཡིག་དྲུག་ཕྱོགས་བཅུར་རྒྱས་པར་ཤོག
SUNG CHOK YIK DRUK CHOK CUR GYE PAR SHOK
And may the supreme speech of your six syllables
pervade the ten directions.

འཕགས་མཆོག་ཁྱེད་ལ་གསོལ་བ་བཏབ་པའི་མཐུས།
PHAK CHOK KHYE LA SÖL WA TAB PE THÜ
Noble and supreme one, by the power of supplicating you,

བདག་གི་གདུལ་བྱར་གྱུར་པའི་འགྲོ་བ་རྣམས།

DAK GI DÜL JAR GYUR PE DRO WA NAM

May beings to be tamed by us

ལས་འབྲས་ལྷུར་ལེན་དགེ་བའི་ལས་ལ་བརྩོན།

LE DRE LHUR LEN GE WE LE LA TSÖN

Practice karma and its result and apply themselves
to virtuous actions.

འགྲོ་བའི་དོན་དུ་ཆོས་དང་ལྡན་པར་ཤོག

DRO WE DÖN DU CHÖ DANG DEN PAR SHOK

May they act in harmony with dharma for the
benefit of beings.

དེ་ལྟར་རྩེ་གཅིག་གསོལ་བཏབ་པས།

DE TAR TSE CIK SÖL TAP PE

Due to our supplicating one-pointedly in that way,

འཕགས་པའི་སྐུ་ལས་འོད་ཟེར་འཕྲོ།

PHAK PE KU LE Ö ZER THRO

Light rays stream forth from the body of the Noble One

མ་དག་ལས་སྣང་འཁྲུལ་ཤེས་སྦྱངས།

MA DAK LE NANG THRÜL SHE JANG

And purify impure karmic appearances
and mistaken consciousness.

ཕྱི་སྣོད་བདེ་བ་ཅན་གྱི་ཞིང་།

CHI NÖ DE WA CEN GYI ZHING

The outer world becomes the pure land of Sukhāvatī.

ནང་བཅུད་སྐྱེ་འགྲོའི་ལུས་ངག་སེམས།

NANG CÜ KYE DRÖ LÜ NGAK SEM

The body, speech, and mind of the inhabitants within

སྤྱན་རས་གཟིགས་དབང་སྐུ་གསུང་ཐུགས།

CEN RE ZI WANG KU SUNG THUK

Become the body, speech, and mind of Avalokita.

སྣང་གྲགས་རིག་སྟོང་དབྱེར་མེད་གྱུར།

NANG DRAK RIK TONG YER ME GYUR

Appearances, sounds, and awareness
are inseparable from emptiness.

While meditating on the meaning of that, recite the mantra as much as you can:

ༀ་མ་ཎི་པདྨེ་ཧཱུྃ།
OM MANI PEME HUNG
OṂ MAṆI PADME HŪṂ

འཁོར་གསུམ་མི་རྟོག་པའི་རང་ངོར་མཉམ་པར་བཞག །
At the end, without conceptualizing the three spheres, rest evenly in your own nature.

བདག་གཞན་ལུས་སྣང་འཕགས་པའི་སྐུ །
DAK ZHEN LÜ NANG PHAK PE KU
The physical appearance of myself and others is the body of the Noble One.

སྒྲ་གྲགས་ཡི་གེ་དྲུག་མའི་དབྱངས།
DRA DRAK YI GE DRUK ME YANG
Sounds are the melody of the six syllables.

དྲན་རྟོག་ཡེ་ཤེས་ཆེན་པོའི་ཀློང་།
DREN TOK YE SHE CHEN PÖ LONG
Thoughts are the expanse of great wisdom.

དགེ་བ་འདི་ཡིས་མྱུར་དུ་བདག
GE WA DI YI NYUR DU DAK
By this merit, may we quickly

སྤྱན་རས་གཟིགས་དབང་འགྲུབ་གྱུར་ནས།
CEN RE ZI WANG DRUP GYUR NE
Accomplish Avalokiteshvara

འགྲོ་བ་གཅིག་ཀྱང་མ་ལུས་པ།
DRO WA CIG KYANG MA LÜ PA
And establish every being without exception

དེ་ཡི་ས་ལ་འགོད་པར་ཤོག
DE YI SA LA GÖ PAR SHOK
In that state.

དེ་ལྟར་སྒོམ་བཟླས་བགྱིས་པའི་བསོད་ནམས་ཀྱིས།
DE TAR GOM DE GYI PE SÖ NAM KYI
By the merit of meditating and reciting in this way,

བདག་དང་བདག་ལ་འབྲེལ་ཐོགས་འགྲོ་བ་ཀུན།

DAK DANG DAK LA DREL THOK DRO WA KÜN
May we and all beings with whom we are connected,

མི་གཙང་ལུས་འདི་བོར་བར་གྱུར་མ་ཐག །

MI TSANG LÜ DI BOR WAR GYUR MA THAK
As soon as we have left behind this impure body,

བདེ་བ་ཅན་དུ་རྫུས་ཏེ་སྐྱེ་བར་ཤོག །

DE WA CEN DU DZÜ TE KYE WAR SHOK
Be miraculously born in Sukhāvatī.

སྐྱེས་མ་ཐག་ཏུ་ས་བཅུ་རབ་བགྲོད་ནས།

KYE MA THAK TU SA CU RAP DRÖ NE
As soon as we are born there, may we traverse
the ten bhūmis

སྤྲུལ་པས་ཕྱོགས་བཅུར་གཞན་དོན་བྱེད་པར་ཤོག །

TRÜL PE CHOK CUR ZHEN DÖN JE PAR CHOK
And benefit others in the ten directions through
our emanations.

དགེ་བ་འདི་ཡིས་སྐྱེ་བོ་ཀུན།

GE WA DI YI KYE WO KUN
By this merit, may all beings

བསོད་ནམས་ཡེ་ཤེས་ཚོགས་རྫོགས་ནས།

SÖ NAM YE SHE TSHOK DZOK NE
Perfect the two accumulations of merit and wisdom

བསོད་ནམས་ཡེ་ཤེས་ལས་བྱུང་བའི།

SÖ NAM YE SHE LE JUNG WE
And achieve the two genuine kāyas

དམ་པ་སྐུ་གཉིས་ཐོབ་པར་ཤོག །

DAM PA KU NYI THOP PAR SHOK
Arising from merit and wisdom.

བྱང་ཆུབ་སེམས་མཆོག་རིན་པོ་ཆེ།

CHANG CHUB SEM CHOK RIN PO CHE
In whomever the precious bodhichitta

མ་སྐྱེས་པ་རྣམས་སྐྱེས་གྱུར་ཅིག །

MA KYE PA NAM KYE GYUR CIG
Has not arisen, may it arise.

སྐྱེས་པ་ཉམས་པ་མེད་པ་དང་།

KYE PA NYAM PA ME PA DANG
In whomever it has arisen, may it not decline,

གོང་ནས་གོང་དུ་འཕེལ་བར་ཤོག །

GONG NE GONG DU PHEL WAR SHOK
But increase further and further.

བདེ་སྨོན་བསྡུས་པ་ནི།
SHORT SUKHĀVATĪ ASPIRATION:

ཨེ་མ་ཧོ༔

E MA HO༔

ངོ་མཚར་སངས་རྒྱས་སྣང་བ་མཐའ་ཡས་དང༔

NGO TSHAR SANG GYE NANG WA THA YE DANG༔
Wondrous buddha Amitābha,༔

གཡས་སུ་ཇོ་བོ་ཐུགས་རྗེ་ཆེན་པོ་དང༔

YE SU JO WO THUK JE CHEN PO DANG༔
On your right, the lord Great Compassionate One,༔

གཡོན་དུ་སེམས་དཔའ་མཐུ་ཆེན་ཐོབ་རྣམས་ལ༔

YÖN DU SEM PA THU CHEN THOP NAM LA༔
On your left, bodhisattva Attainer of Great Power,༔

སངས་རྒྱས་བྱང་སེམས་དཔག་མེད་འཁོར་གྱིས་སྐོར༔

SANG GYE CHANG SEM PAK ME KHOR GYI KOR༔
Surrounded by a retinue of countless buddhas
and bodhisattvas.༔

བདེ་སྐྱིད་ངོ་མཚར་དཔག་ཏུ་མེད་པ་ཡི༔

DE KYI NGO TSHAR PAK TU ME PA YI༔
In this buddhafield known as Sukhāvatī༔

བདེ་བ་ཅན་ཞེས་བྱ་བའི་ཞིང་ཁམས་དེར༔

DE WA CEN ZHE JA WE ZHING KHAM DER༔
Of wondrous, boundless joy and happiness,༔

བདག་ནི་འདི་ནས་ཚེ་འཕོས་གྱུར་མ་ཐག༔

DAK NI DI NE TSHE PHÖ GYUR MA THAK༔

May we be born, as soon as we depart from this life,༔

སྐྱེ་བ་གཞན་གྱི་བར་མ་ཆོད་པ་རུ༔

KYE WA ZHEN GYI BAR MA CHÖ PA RU༔

Not taking other births in between,༔

དེ་རུ་སྐྱེས་ནས་སྣང་མཐའི་ཞལ་མཐོང་ཤོག༔

DE RU KYE NE NANG THE ZHAL THONG SHOK༔

And see the face of Amitābha.༔

དེ་སྐད་བདག་གིས་སྨོན་ལམ་བཏབ་པ་འདི༔

DE KE DAK GI MÖN LAM TAP PA DI༔

May all the buddhas and bodhisattvas
of the ten directions༔

ཕྱོགས་བཅུའི་སངས་རྒྱས་བྱང་སེམས་ཐམས་ཅད་ཀྱིས༔

CHOK CÜ SANG GYE CHANG SEM THAM CE KYI༔

Grant their blessings so that our aspiration༔

གེགས་མེད་འགྲུབ་པར་བྱིན་གྱིས་བརླབ་ཏུ་གསོལ༔

GEK ME DRUP PAR JIN GYI LAP TU SÖL༔

May be accomplished without obstruction.༔

ཏདྱ་ཐཱ༔ པཉྩེནྡྲི་ཡ་ཨ་ཝ་བོ་དྷ་ནི་ཡེ་སྭཱ་ཧཱ༔

TEYATHA PENTSENDRIYA AWABODANIYE SO HA༔

TAD YATHĀ PAÑCHANDRIYA AVABHODANĪYE SVĀHĀ༔

The root text was written by the Shangpa siddha Thangtong Gyalpo. The seven-branch prayer and Supplication of Calling with Longing were written by Pema Karpo. The Abbreviated Sukhāvatī Supplication is a terma received by Mingyur Dorje.

The Benefit of Others That Fills All of Space

by Jamgon Kongtrul

The Benefit of Others That Fills All of Space

The Method for Conferring the Reading Transmission of the Meditation of the Six Syllables from the Direct Lineage of the Lord of Siddhas, the Great Iron Bridge Builder[4]

Namo Lokeshvaraya
Father who protects the destitute beings of this polluted age,
Lord of the world who bears the name Diligence,
To you and the guru, the protector of beings
Who holds the treasury of your instructions, I prostrate.
Now I shall explain the reading transmission of Avalokita—
The special teaching of the Great Siddha,
The essence of the instructions that shake saṃsāra from its depths,
And the heart of the eighty thousand gates of dharma.

Here, you spiritual teachers who have entered the path of excellent conduct, which makes all connections meaningful, should recall with certainty in your hearts the benefits of merely hearing the teachings and be free of discriminating amongst those of supreme or lesser fortune. With the good-heart intention of bodhichitta and a desire beyond mundane hopes and material concerns to give the generosity of dharma, take your seat on the dharma throne in the center of the assembly. If possible, practice your own abbreviated meditation and recitation. After that, address the assembly as follows.

So that those who have been our mothers, all sentient beings limitless as space, may attain complete, perfect buddhahood, first develop a pure motivation: think that for that very purpose you will listen to, and correctly put into practice, this profound reading transmission for the meditation on the six syllables. Adopt an outlook that sees this very place as the pure realm of Sukhāvatī and the teacher as being Avalokita in person. Having fixed your body in a respectful posture

4. "Lord of Siddhas," "Great Siddha," and "Iron Bridge Builder" are here all epithets of Thangtong Gyalpo.

with your hands in *añjali* [5] and so on, having abandoned frivolity in speech, and with your mind not distracted toward other things, please listen with one-pointed respect to this genuine dharma and its teacher, the spiritual friend.

The Lord of Siddhas Thangtong Gyalpo, whose name's renown rivals that of the sun and moon, was the noble and supreme Avalokita and Padmākara inseparable, emanated as a practitioner of yogic conduct. Once, when young, he led a ritual for the accumulation of one hundred million recitations of the six-syllable mantra. At that time, the dawn of the eighth day of the month of Magical Illusion,[6] the brim ornament of the vase sitting before him transformed into a great wish-fulfilling tree.

In the midst of the branches and leaves that stemmed from its trunk were four seats made of lotuses and moon discs, one above the other. On each seat from lowest to highest, there in the midst of a luminous maṇḍala stood noble Avalokita in the forms of Khasarpaṇi, the Four-Armed, the Eight-Armed, and the Thousand-Armed-Thousand-Eyed, each body adorned with the major and minor marks. Along the edges of the maṇḍala were Hayagriva, Amṛitakundali, Tārā, Ushnisha Vijayi, and the buddhas of the ten directions. The maṇḍala's lower section was encircled by the Guardians of the Ten Directions, the Twelve Yakshas, and the Four Great Kings.

Seeing this directly, Thangtong Gyalpo offered the seven-branch prayer and other supplications, to which Avalokita responded, "O child of noble family, as I am your master until you attain enlightenment, perform vast activity by means of the six syllables and be a guide to beings!"

The essence of the many instructions that Avalokita directly bestowed upon him at that time is this meditation and recitation of the six syllables, profound yet easy to practice. The conferring and practice of its reading transmission has three parts:

1. The preliminaries: refuge and bodhichitta, which turn one's mind toward the dharma
2. The main practice: creation, recitation, and completion, done in connection with the meditation practice *All-Pervading Benefit of Beings*
3. The conclusion: dedicating the roots of virtue to the benefit of others in connection with the three outlooks

5. A gesture of joining the palms of one's hands at the level of the chest.
6. The first Tibetan month, called "Chotrül" (*cho 'phrul*). It is called the month of "Magical Illusion" because during this month the historical Buddha, Shākyamuni, displayed various miracles, causing his teachings to spread throughout the land of India.

1. The preliminaries: refuge and bodhichitta, which turn one's mind toward the dharma

In the sky in front of you, on a jewel throne and a lotus and moon disc seat, is your own root guru in essence, appearing in the form of Avalokita that is known as the Four-Armed Tamer of Beings. He is surrounded by a retinue of innumerable buddhas and bodhisattvas. In their presence, think that yourself and others, all sentient beings, from this day forward until you have attained perfect enlightenment, take refuge from the bottom of your hearts. Apply this one-pointed focus to the stanza of refuge below, the uncommon refuge of the Iron Bridge Builder known as "the nine-fold refuge."[7] It was taught by the Great Compassionate One to Ka-ngapa Paljor Sherab and then given as a transmission to the Great Siddha. It contains blessings that are rich in experience and accomplishment. Concentrating on the visualizations explained above, recite together this verse of refuge:

Those who have been my mothers, all sentient beings, limitless as space,
take refuge in the guru, the precious Buddha.
We take refuge in the Buddha, dharma and saṅgha.
We take refuge in the assemblies of gurus, yidams, and ḍākinīs.
We take refuge in our minds, emptiness-clarity, the dharmakāya.

When conferring the reading transmission for this practice, you may say this and all of the verses that appear below either three or seven times by chanting them together with the students or by having them repeat after you.

Say that 108, twenty-one, or seven times, as time permits. The objects of refuge then melt into light and dissolve into you. Thereby, think that the blessings of the compassionate ones have entered you, that your mind naturally turns toward the dharma, and that all obstacles have been removed.

In the phase following that, reflect in this way:

"Oh, these poor sentient beings, my mothers and fathers, limitless as space! Continuously, they wander in saṃsāra, this ocean of suffering. I alone must place them all in the state of complete buddhahood. As I do not now have that ability, I will practice the essence of all dharmas—the meditation and recitation of the six syllables—and will quickly liberate sentient beings."

7. The enumeration of the nine-fold refuge is as follows: 1. one's guru, 2. the Buddha (from whom one's guru is viewed as inseparable), 3. the (historical) Buddha, 4. the dharma, 5. the sangha, 6. the gurus, 7. the yidams, 8. the ḍākinīs, 9. the dharmakāya.

With this attitude of captain- or shepherd-like bodhichitta,[8] recite the following:

> So that all sentient beings may attain the state of complete, perfect buddhahood,
> I will practice the meditation and recitation of the noble Great Compassionate One.

Say that several times, making certain that a wholesome and uplifted intention has mixed with your mindstream.

Taking refuge in the beginning becomes the basis for taking all further vows. It turns one's mind toward the dharma and ensures that obstacles to practicing the path will not arise. Engendering bodhichitta ensures that whatever thought or deed one engages in from then on will become an aid to enlightenment. Therefore, these two are necessary for one's dharma practice to become successful.

Urging one's mind toward the dharma through introspective contemplation is divided into three parts:

1.1. Laying the ground of renunciation
1.2. Snapping the whip of exertion
1.3. Making the link[9] with shepherd-like bodhichitta

1.1. Laying the ground of renunciation

This is divided into two parts:

1.1.1. The general analysis
1.1.2. The specific analysis

1.1.1. The general analysis

Since beginningless time, the six kinds of beings have taken as a self that which is devoid of self. This ignorance, along with the conditions of karma and mental afflictions, is the cause that produces beings. When the appearances of each type of being are analyzed, they are found to be like the friends and enemies seen in a dream, or like an illusory kingdom: in these appearances, not even a speck of dust exists from its own side.

Nevertheless, confused appearances are taken to be real, and the three sufferings arise: all-pervasive suffering, filled with mental afflictions and latent habitual tendencies; the suffering of change, seeming happiness that quickly fades with impermanence; and the suffering of suffering, the direct experience of the results of negative actions.

8. These are two of the three ways of engendering bodhichitta (Tib. *sems bskyed gsum*/"*semkye sum*"). With captain-like bodhichitta, one wishes to guide all sentient beings to enlightenment, bringing them to that fruition simultaneously with one's own enlightenment. With shepherd-like bodhichitta, one wishes to help all sentient beings attain enlightenment so that oneself attains enlightenment last, after each and every sentient being has first gained liberation. The third way to engender bodhichitta, not mentioned here, is king-like bodhichitta, wherein one aspires to first attain enlightenment for oneself and thereafter work to liberate all sentient beings without exception.
9. Tib. *mtshams sbyar ba*/"*tsham jarwa*"

Just as the sesame is pervaded by oil, so the sentient beings of the six classes and three realms do not pass beyond these three great sufferings. Here in saṃsāra there is no happiness, not even the measure of a tip of a strand of hair. Considering this, fervently give rise to renunciation.

1.1.2. The specific analysis

Regarding the analysis of each of the six classes, the *Sūtra on the Establishment of Mindfulness*[10] says:

> Beings of hell fall[11] in hellish fires;
> Hungry ghosts fall in thirst and hunger.
> Animals fall through eating one another,
> And gods fall through carelessness.
> Jealous gods fall in fighting,
> And humans fall with lives so short.
> Never is even a needle's tip of joy
> Found in saṃsāra.

Accordingly, from the peak of existence down to the Avīchi hell,[12] whether born in a high or low level of saṃsāra, one will experience only suffering. Therefore, just as one would abandon food that has been mixed with poison, regardless of whatever good or bad appearances it may have, so should a mind of renunciation, a mind of definite emergence from saṃsāra, be fervently engendered.

1.2. Snapping the whip of exertion

From among all of these forms of existence, now examine in particular the condition of us humans. If one has not been born into any of the eight situations of no-leisure, one possesses the eight freedoms.[13] To have these, as well as the five advantages from one's own perspective[14] and the five advantages from the perspective of others,[15] is to be endowed with the "eighteen freedoms and advantages." Such a human body is very hard to find. Further, if obtained, it is of

10. Tib. *sdo sde dran pa nyer bzhag*/"do-de drenpa nyer-shak"
11. The Tibetan word translated by "fall" in this verse is "nyam" (*nyams*), which literally means "to decline" or "to degenerate." The English word "fall" was chosen here for its evocative quality.
12. The Avîchi hell is the lowest and most unpleasant of the many hell realms taught in traditional Buddhist cosmology.
13. The eight freedoms (Tib. *dal ba brgyad*/"*dalwa gye*") are the states free of the eight states of no-leisure (Tib. *mi khom pa brgyad*/"*mi khompa gye*"). Thus, these freedoms consist of freedom from: 1) the hell realms, 2) the hungry ghost realms, 3) the animal realms, 4) barbaric existences, 5) being a long-living god, 6) having wrong views, 7) being born into a place where there has never been a buddha, and 8) having inadequate intellectual faculties.
14. Tib. *rang 'byor lnga*/"*rangjor nga*": 1) being a human, 2) being born in a central land, 3) having all five sense faculties, 4) not having extreme karmic burdens, and 5) having faith in the three collections of the Buddha's teaching.
15. Tib. *gzhan 'byor lnga*/"*shenjor nga*": Being born where: 1) a buddha has arrived, 2) the buddha has taught the dharma, 3) the dharma has survived, 4) one has entered into those teachings, 5) conditions are favorable for the practice of dharma.

immense benefit and is therefore similar in quality to a precious jewel. The difficulty of obtaining such a human birth can be illustrated by way of causes, examples, and numbers. While there are as many beings of the lower realms as there are atoms in the whole earth, there are only as many humans as there are atoms on the tip of a fingernail. Still, these are merely ordinary human bodies. A human body that is suitable for the dharma is as rare as a daytime star. *The Compassionate White Lotus Sūtra*[16] says:

> Human birth is hard to find.
> Abundance of freedom is hard to find.
> A buddha appearing in the world is hard to find.
> Desire for virtuous qualities is hard to find.
> Pure aspiration prayers, as well, are hard to find.

Limitless statements like that have been made. However, even if one obtains a human body as described above, one will still not have transcended the four great rivers of birth, aging, sickness, and death, and will thus enjoy not even an instant of permanence or happiness.

In general, all conditioned things are subject to the "four ends" of impermanent phenomena: the end of being together is parting; the end of accumulation is exhaustion; the end of being high is being low; the end of birth is certainly dying. In particular, the time of death for a human body is uncertain, and there is no way one can be sure about how death will come. Like a prisoner awaiting execution, with each passing night one comes closer to death. Like a water bubble, an avalanche off a steep mountain, or lightning in the sky, death will quickly and suddenly befall us. Whatever it may be—neither scholarship, righteousness, power, wealth, heroism, physical strength, divinations, rituals, nor medical examinations will avail—it cannot turn death away.

Your consciousness, unaccompanied by any of your possessions, authority or fame, will associate only with your positive and negative karma as it travels to the place of your next life. At that time, through your negative actions, you will fall to the lower realms; or, though your virtuous actions, you will proceed to the higher realms and the attainment of liberation.

Since this is the case, there is nothing besides the genuine dharma that will be of benefit to your future lives. Leave alone the next life; for this life too it is only the dharma that brings great benefit, both immediately and in the long term. Therefore, not delaying until tomorrow or the next day, from this very moment onward develop the three kinds of faith:

16. Tib. *snying rje pad ma dkar po'i mdo*/"*nyingje pema karpö do*"

trusting faith in karma and its result, lucid faith in the guru and the three jewels, and longing faith toward the accomplishment of enlightenment. Endowed with these three, settle your mind on an attitude that sees your body as a servant and vessel. Make a firm oath that you will strive only toward the genuine dharma.

1.3. Making the link with shepherd-like bodhichitta

Think in this way:

"Oh, dear! For the brief while that I have this human body, this apparition that is like a daytime star, however I act in body shall accomplish vast virtue. Whatever I utter in speech will encourage the purity of helping others. Whatever I think in mind will be virtuous and inclusive of all sentient beings." Develop vast thoughts and actions in this way, with body, speech, and mind harnessed toward the benefit of sentient beings. "To accomplish those ends, I supplicate the manifestation of the compassion of all buddhas, the special deity for the Snowy Land of Tibet, the lord Great Compassionate One." Thinking in this way, begin the visualizations for *All-Pervading Benefit of Beings.*

2. The main practice

2.1. Creation stage meditation
2.2. Recitation
2.3. Completion stage meditation

2.1. Creation stage meditation

On the crown of your head and those of others, all sentient beings of the six realms, on a white lotus and moon disc seat, is HRĪḤ. From it is born the supreme noble Avalokiteshvara, his body white in color like an autumn moon, translucent like the water-crystal jewel, and radiating stainless light rays of five colors.

Because all phenomena are of one taste in suchness, he has one face. Because his loving-kindness embraces all, his smile shines in all directions. Because his pure eyes behold all throughout the six phases,[17] they open as utterly wide as the leaves of the Utpala flower.[18]

Because he urges the buddhas of the ten directions and three times to perform the benefit of beings, his first two hands are joined in añjali at his heart center. As a symbol of his compassion being unceasing, his second right hand holds a māla of white crystal, telling its 108 beads. Because he is not covered by the mud of self-centered thinking, his left hand holds

17. Three phases of the daytime and three phases of the night. "The six phases" is a phrase used to convey a sense of continuity, i.e., "All the time."
18. The blue lotus

a fully blossomed eight-petaled white lotus by the stem, adjacent to his left ear.

His skirt, made of fine cloth that is of the character of shame and modesty, is adorned by a jewel-encrusted waist-belt. Because compassion and emptiness are inseparable, he is seated with his legs in the vajra posture. Representing the eight forms of liberation,[19] he is adorned with the eight precious ornaments.[20] Because he possesses the elegance of great compassion, his left breast is covered by a cloth of deerskin.

Because he exemplifies an object of supplication, his guru Amitābha beautifies the topknot of his hair.

Because the cooling rays of his great compassion pacify the blistering heat of the mental afflictions, his back is supported by a stainless full moon.

Imagining that you, along with all sentient beings of the six realms, are supplicating with great respect the essence of the root and lineage gurus and the assemblies of yidam deities and all buddhas and bodhisattvas combined, recite this:

> Lord, white in color, unstained by faults,
> A perfect buddha adorning your head,
> You look upon beings with eyes of compassion.
> Avalokita, we prostrate to you.

Chant that supplication as many times as you can. Then, if you wish, you may chant the vajra speech supplication, rich in blessings, that was made to Avalokita by the Siddha when he took birth as the bhikṣhu Pema Karpo, as well as supplications to the lineage.

2.2. Recitation

Through your having supplicated in that way, limitless light rays emanate from the body of the Noble One on the crown of your head. They fill the environment and its inhabitants, purifying the impure manifestations of karmic appearances. The container, the world, becomes a palace, and its inhabitants, all sentient beings, are transformed to abide within the three maṇḍalas of appearance, sound and thought.

Their bodies, appearance-emptiness inseparable, are of the nature of the body of the Noble One. Their speech, sound-emptiness inseparable, is the innate resonance of the six syllables. Their minds, awareness-emptiness inseparable, are the play of primordial wisdom. With one-pointed focus, recite the six syllables together within this pervasive samādhi that extends throughout the reaches of space.

19. The eight forms of liberation (Tib. *rnam thar brgyad*/"*namthar gye*") are: 1) the liberation of regarding what has form to be form, 2) the liberation of regarding the formless as having form, 3) the liberation of the repulsive and clearing away hindrances, 4, 5, 6, and 7) the four liberations of the four formless states, and 8) the liberation of cessation.

20. The eight precious ornaments (Tib. *rin po che'i rgyan brgyad*/"*rinpochey gyen gye*") are: 1) crown, 2) earrings, 3) short necklace, 4) medium necklace, 5) long necklace, 6) arm bracelets, 7) ankle bracelets, 8) belt.

OṂ MAṆI PADME HŪṂ

During the recitation section of the reading transmission, the six-syllable mantra is traditionally chanted 108 or however many times are appropriate.

Recite the six syllables for as long as you can.

2.3. Completion stage meditation

At the end of the meditation and recitation, look at your mind—emptiness-clarity, endowed with an essence of awareness. It is the dharmatā, the ultimate Great Compassionate One, the natural presence of the three kāyas there from the beginning, the very face of buddha nature pervading all stages of ground, path, and fruition. With innate awareness free of viewer and viewed, look nakedly.

Free from the discursive pursuits of altering, accepting, and rejecting, let go of attachment toward experiences of bliss, clarity, non-thought, and so on. Cut completely the movement of mind that clings to forms. Though thoughts may arise and disperse, allow them to free themselves within the self-pacified, innate dharmatā. Rest evenly for as long as you can in the true nature, simplicity.

3. The subsequent activities

If you wish to arise from that equipoise, imagine again that your body appears as that of the Noble One, yet without any inherent nature. Do not engage in accepting and rejecting motivated by lust, hatred, and dullness towards sentient beings—friends, enemies, and those who are neutral. Instead, resolve that all appearances are of the nature of the body of the Noble One, that all sounds are the naturally resounding six syllables, and that any thoughts that arise of good and bad are great primordial wisdom. Without relishing thoughts, rest starkly[21] in the bare essence of whatever appears.

Maintaining this yoga of the three outlooks, motivate yourself with unbiased loving-kindness and compassion toward your mothers and fathers, sentient beings who take confused appearances to be real. In an illusion-like way that does not cling to things as real, exert yourself in as much virtue as possible in body, speech, and mind.

Then, with the supreme practitioner having purified the three spheres[22], the middling practitioner with an illusion-like mind, and the lesser practitioner with an intention of following in the footsteps of the victorious ones and their heirs, recite together this dedication to all sentient beings of the roots of virtue:

21. Tib. *he de ba*/"*hedewa*"

22. This refers to being free of perceiving as truly existent the three aspects of any given action: the actor, the object of the action, and the action itself.

By the roots of virtue accumulated in this way,
may we and our mothers and fathers,
all sentient beings, attain buddhahood.

Also,

By this virtue, may we quickly
Accomplish Avalokiteshvara
And establish all beings without exception
In that state.

In this way, through sincere dedication prayers, seal the practice.

You have now listened well to this reading transmission throughout its profound stages. This meditation and recitation when received by supreme practitioners will be practiced continually throughout the four sessions, by middling practitioners every day without fail, and by common practitioners once a week. The benefits of such practice, spoken of in the sūtras, tantras, and treatises, cannot be properly conveyed using words. Nonetheless, among them are the purification of misdeeds, obscurations, and mental afflictions, the arising of compassion and realization, the accomplishment of vast benefit for others, and, subsequent to rebirth in Sukhāvatī in one's next life, the swift attainment of buddhahood. Therefore, these instructions accomplish great benefit with little difficulty.

The benefit for oneself is accomplished through practicing one-pointedly. Explaining and propagating this practice to others, or even uttering the name of the Great Compassionate One or the six syllables in the ears of creatures from ants upward, will accomplish the benefit of others. Thus, this noble path spontaneously accomplishes the two benefits, shaking saṃsāra from its depths and benefiting all those with whom it comes into contact. Please bring it to completion.

By this merit, may we attain omniscience
And thus defeat the enemy, wrongdoing.
From the stormy waves of birth, old age, sickness and death,
From the ocean of saṃsāra, may we free all beings.

Thus, close with short dedication prayers.

Through simply bringing this meditation and recitation to mind,
May the actions of immediate retribution and all obscurations be exhausted.
In particular, through this explanation of the practice instructions
Of the only protector of the Land of Snows,
Through seeing, hearing, recalling and touching,
May all beings be confirmed by the protector of the world
In the pure realm of Limitless Light.
May all of his legacies be accomplished.

Recalling in the lotus of my heart the ambrosial speech-rays of Mañjugosha, the one endowed with non-referential compassion, this, the heart intention of all the old root texts, has been elucidated by the six-syllable reciter Lodrö Thaye by condensing the pith written instructions of the Iron Bridge Builder, like mother and son. It was written with pure intention at the hermitage of Palpung. May the benefit that it brings to others equal space. May virtue and goodness increase!

The Continuous Rain of Benefit to Beings

by the 15th Karmapa, Khakhyab Dorje

The Continuous Rain of Benefit to Beings

An Abbreviated Annotation of All-Pervading Benefit of Beings, the Meditation and Recitation of the Supreme Noble Avalokiteshvara

Svasti
Arising as the expression
Of the great compassion of all victorious ones,
Avalokita, your activity shakes saṃsāra from its depths.
To you, inseparable from the venerable lord,[23] *I bow.*

His noble heart and enlightened activity exceed that of all other victorious ones. For as long as saṃsāra has not been emptied, he does not remain absorbed in the samādhi of peace, but throughout the continuum of the three times eternally performs the activity of guiding the six classes of beings.

In particular, in accordance with the enthronement and prophecy he received from the Victorious One, Friend of the Sun,[24] he took on as his noble realm of disciples the country of the red-faced ones, the land of the extremely difficult-to-tame.[25] There, he directly performed enlightened activity through assuming various forms, such as those of kings, ministers, translators, scholars, yogic adepts, and young boys and girls.

The power of his blessing is illustrated by children who know how to say his six syllables, the king of secret mantras, from the time they can talk, without ever learning it from anyone. There is no special deity for the Land of Snows other than this lord, the Great Compassionate One.

23. "Venerable lord" (Tib. *rje btsun*/"*jetsün*") is a reference to the author's root guru.
24. "Friend of the Sun" (Tib. *nyi ma'i gnyen*/"*nyi-mey nyen*") is an epithet for the Buddha Shākyamuni.
25. A reference to Tibet.

The supreme beings of the past who were his emanations wrote clearly a limitless number of texts, both elaborate and condensed in form, that deal with the practice of the Noble One. From among these, our text here is called *All-Pervading Benefit of Beings*.[26] It was handed down to us by the Lord of Siddhas Thangtong Gyalpo, who was actually Avalokita in person, emanated for the benefit of humans. The explanation of its practice is presented under the following headings.

1. The preparation
1.1. Refuge and bodhichitta

2. The main practice
2.1. Meditating on the deity
2.2. Reciting the mantra

3. The subsequent activities
3.1. Implementing the practice in daily life
3.2. Dedicating the roots of virtue

4. The teaching on the benefits

1.1. Refuge and bodhichitta

In the space before you, in an expanse filled with cloudbanks of rainbow lights and flowers, is Avalokita, inseparable from your root guru, vividly present as the essence of the three jewels and three roots, all victorious ones combined. In front of him, led by you, are all sentient beings of the six realms: friends, enemies, and those who are neutral. You are all gathered together with body, speech, and mind acting in unison.

Because guru Avalokita has the ability and power to protect you from saṃsāra, the great ocean of suffering, develop therefore faith that completely casts away all other hopes and objects of reliance, longing that calls out for his protection, and trust in such protection being certain. Possessed of these three, recite:

In the supreme Buddha, dharma and assembly,
I take refuge until attaining enlightenment.

Saying that as many times as is suitable, go for refuge. Give rise to unmoving certainty that from now onward you and all sentient beings have been placed under the protection of the noble Great Compassionate One.

Now, turn your focus toward the sentient beings visualized in front of you and think:

"Of all these beings, there is not even one who has not been my kind mother or father. Although they wish only to enjoy happiness and shun suffering, they have practiced only the causes of suffering. As a result, they are tormented without a

26. Tib. *'gro don mkha' khyab ma*/"*drodön kha-khyabma*"

moment's release by the severe sufferings of the lower realms of saṃsāra. I must by all means establish them in the most supreme of all forms of happiness, the unsurpassable state of complete buddhahood. Because I do not now have the ability to do this, I will practice the profound meditation and recitation of the noble Avalokita and thereby attain the genuine state of this supreme Noble One. For as long as saṃsāra remains, I will engage for the benefit of beings in conduct that measures up to Avalokita's example."

In the presence of guru Avalokita, with this genuine and fervent aspiration, take on the oath of engendering bodhichitta, the mind set on enlightenment, by reciting as follows:

> Through the merit of practicing meditation and recitation,
> May I attain buddhahood in order to benefit beings.[27]

Saying that a few times, develop clear certainty as to the purpose of this meditation.

Then multiple light rays stream forth from the body of guru Avalokita. They strike the visualized sentient beings, purifying their misdeeds, obscurations, and suffering, and establishing them in happiness. The objects of refuge then melt into light and dissolve into you. As they do, think that your mindstream becomes blessed.

2.1. Meditating on the deity

Surrounding you as you sit in your ordinary form are the objects of compassion, the six classes of beings, visualized as at the time of going for refuge. On the crown of your head and those of others is a fully blossomed white eight-petaled lotus with anthers. At its center on a stainless full moon disc is the syllable HRĪḤ, white and shining like a pearl. Meditate that it is the direct expression of the power of all victorious ones condensed into a single form.

From it streams limitless light like the rays of the moon. The light makes pleasing offerings of body, speech, and mind to all maṇḍalas of the victorious ones of the ten directions without exception.

As the light strikes yourself and others, it purifies all illness, negative energies, misdeeds, and obscurations. Pervading the abodes of the six classes of beings, it dispels beings' suffering and establishes them in happiness. The blessings of the assemblies of noble ones are then gathered back in the form of light rays. These dissolve into the HRĪḤ syllables above your head and those of others, where in an instant there appears Avalokiteshvara, his body utterly white in color like a sunrise shining on the snow.

27. The standard version of this line of the verse reads, "Through the merit of practicing generosity and so on," (Tib. *bdag gis sbyin sogs bgyis pa'i bsod nams kyis*/"*dak gi jin sok gyi pe sö nam kyi*"). However, it is common to alter this line to make it accord with the activity one is about to engage in, as is done here.

From his body, lucid and radiant, stream forth light rays of five colors, which pervade the pure realms of the victorious ones. In this way, he urges the noble ones to perform the benefit of beings. Below him, the light rays pervade the abodes of the six classes of beings. The suffering of each and every being is washed away, and they are established in happiness.

Showing that he is pleased, Avalokita's smile shines toward you and all sentient beings. His two eyes look upon sentient beings continually throughout the three times; his gaze always reflects his heart, which cares for and loves all beings, oneself and others, just as a mother loves her only child. He has four arms; the first two are joined in añjali at his heart center, his lower right hand holds a māla of white crystal, and his lower left hand holds by its stem an eight-petaled lotus.

He is beautifully clothed in a silk scarf and an upper garment of white silk with golden embroidery. He wears a skirt of red cloth. His crown, earrings, short, middle, and long necklaces, shoulder ornaments, and bracelets on his arms and ankles are all made of gold from the Jambu River, adorned with many heaps of the precious stones of the gods. Sweet-sounding music resonates from his waist belt, a garland of small bells. Thus, all parts of his body are well ornamented.

His left breast is covered by the yellow skin of the Krishnasari deer. The hair that is not tied up in his topknot flows freely down his back. His head is ornamented by the lord of his family,[28] the supreme buddha Amitābha, who is dressed in nirmāṇakāya form and seated in the vajra posture. Behind Avalokita is a stainless and utterly full moon.

Thinking that he is the embodiment of all the rare and supreme objects of refuge that appear throughout the three times and dwell in the ten directions, recite the following:

On the crown of my head and those of others, sentient beings pervading space,
On a white lotus and moon,
From HRĪḤ, appears noble and supreme Avalokita.
He is brilliant white and radiates the five lights.
Handsome and smiling, he looks on with eyes of compassion.
He has four hands: the first are joined in añjali;
The lower two hold a crystal māla and a white lotus.
Adorned with ornaments of silks and jewels,
He wears an upper garment of deerskin.
Amitābha crowns his head.
His two feet are in the vajra posture.
His back rests against a stainless moon.
He is the embodiment of all objects of refuge.

Read slowly and divide the text into sections, clearly visualizing each aspect of his body.

28. There are five "Buddha families." The Buddha family to which Avalokita belongs is the Padma family, the central Buddha of which is Amitābha.

2.2. Reciting the mantra

This has two parts: 2.2.1. Invoking the enlightened heart through supplication
2.2.2. Practicing the deity yoga of the three gates through emanating and gathering

2.2.1. Invoking the enlightened heart through supplication

Supplicate Avalokita, visualized as described above, in this way: "Supreme noble one, guru Avalokita, I and all sentient beings, with one voice and with one-pointed mind, have cast away all other objects of reliance and completely entrust ourselves to you. Please liberate the six classes of beings from their saṃsāric existences and lead us to the state of omniscience." Thinking in this way, recite:

Lord, white in color, unstained by faults,
A perfect buddha adorning your head,
You look upon beings with eyes of compassion.
Avalokita, we prostrate to you.

Saying that one hundred, twenty-one, or seven times, invoke his mindstream. Recite until certainty arises that your perceptions have changed.

If you wish and are able, insert other prayers that carry blessings, such as the *"Po" Praise*[29] of Bhikṣhunī Lakṣhmī[30] and the *Lamenting Praise*[31] of the master Chandrakīrti.[32] Adding supplications of any kind that carry blessings will undoubtedly become a worthy extension.

2.2.2. Practicing the deity yoga of the three gates through emanating and gathering

Through your supplicating and invoking his heart with such one-pointed mind, limitless light rays of five colors, with white predominant, radiate from the body of the Noble One seated on the crown of your head. Through their merely coming into contact with you and all sentient beings, they purify everything that has accumulated in your mindstream since beginningless time, as the light of a torch dispels darkness.

As to what is purified, this includes the five acts of immediate consequence,[33] as well as the three non-virtuous actions

29. So called because most of the lines in the Tibetan version of the praise have as their last syllable "*po*," which means, "the one who..."

30. Tib. *dge slong ma dpal mo*/"*Gelongma Palmo*." An Indian woman who lived around the tenth and eleventh centuries. She was a fully ordained nun who realized perfect accomplishment in the practice of Avalokiteshvara and composed a liturgy for the practice of "*Nyung-ne*," the fasting retreat practice associated with the Eleven-Faced, Eleven-Armed Avalokiteshvara.

31. Tib. *smre ngag gi bstod pa*/"*me-ngag gi töpa*"

32. Chandrakīrti was an Indian master of the late sixth/early seventh century. He is primarily known for his great expositions on the topic of Madhyamaka or Middle Way philosophy, the tradition founded by the master Nāgārjuna.

33. Tib. *mtshams med lnga*/"*tsham me nga*." The five acts of immediate consequence are five types of actions whose karmic consequences are said to ripen in the same lifetime as that in which the action was committed. The five are: 1) matricide, 2) patricide, 3) killing an arhat, 4) inciting a schism in the sangha, and 5) with malicious intent, drawing blood from the body of a buddha.

of body—taking life, taking what is not offered, and sexual misconduct; the four non-virtuous actions of speech—lying (making statements that harm one's guru and others, such as boasting of qualities one does not possess), inciting discord (creating rifts between others), harsh speech (which hurts others' feelings), and idle chatter (which is simply meaningless); and the three non-virtuous actions of mind—covetousness (mentally scheming about obtaining the wealth of others), malicious intent (thinking of methods with which to harm others), and wrong view (viewing the benefits of liberation and the shortcomings of misdeeds as untrue and nonexistent). These are the ten non-virtuous actions, and they, along with the actions that are conducive to them, are misdeeds.[34]

There are also the actions committed out of passion, hatred, ignorance, pride, and jealousy that have been prescribed in the ethical codes as things to be abandoned, or, even though not so prescribed, naturally fall into the category of moral faults. Since these obscure the attainment of the happiness of the higher realms and liberation, they are called obscurations.[35]

Then there are the downfalls[36]—instances in which one has taken on the vows of individual liberation, bodhichitta, or secret mantra, and does not guard them due to disrespect or carelessness. They are called "downfalls" because, through committing them, one will fall down to the lower realms.

There are also other forms of wrongdoings, such as the transgressions of subtle points of training, which may not cause one to fall to the lower realms, but nonetheless delay the attainment of enlightenment.

All of these impurities—whatever wrongdoings[37] and downfalls there are that have been produced by the negative karma of misdeeds, obscurations, and mental afflictions—are, in the very instant of the light contacting yourself and others, purified.

The light rays also cleanse the knowledge obscurations and habitual tendencies that from beginningless time have supported dualistic clinging to the confused appearances of self and other. Beings are blessed into the experience of inseparability from the body, speech, and mind of noble Avalokita. The form of the Noble One, appearing yet empty, like a rainbow, becomes increasingly vivid.

The light rays pervade the abodes of the six classes of beings, limitless as space, causing the vessels of external worlds and all objects that appear within them to become the pure realm of Akaniṣhṭha Sukhāvatī. Free of even the names of rocks, mountains, and cliffs, its forms are of the nature of precious jewels and spheres of rainbow light.

The inhabitants, each and every sentient being of the six realms, are freed from their suffering, and the bodies of all beings suddenly become the body of the noble Great Compassionate One. The speech of beings, along with all the sounds of the elements, is the self-sounding melody of the secret six-syllable mantra. Conceptuality, the confused aspect of mind, is purified; and beings realize the mind of the Noble One, the heart of inseparable awareness and emptiness. Meditate that all of this has become so.

34. Tib. *sdig pa*/"*dikpa*"
35. Tib. *sgrib pa*/"*dribpa*"
36. Tib. *ltung ba*/"*tungwa*"
37. Tib. *nyes pa*/"*nyepa*"

In this way, the pure appearances of kāyas and pure realms, the sound of the secret mantra, and the naked mind of awareness-emptiness are inseparable from the appearances of the body, speech, and mind of yourself and all others. While resting free of fixation in this great all-pervasiveness beyond intellect, recite the following:

Due to our supplicating one-pointedly in that way,
Light rays stream forth from the body of the Noble One
And purify impure karmic appearances and mistaken consciousness.
The outer world becomes the pure land of Sukhāvatī.
The body, speech, and mind of the inhabitants within
Become the body, speech, and mind of Avalokita.
Appearances, sounds, and awareness are inseparable from emptiness.

Then, maintaining the visualizations explained above, recite this mantra as the main practice:

OṂ MAṆI PADME HŪṂ

This secret mantra, the six syllables, is the embodiment of the energy and power of all the compassion and activity of noble Avalokita, who is himself the embodiment of the wisdom energy of all buddhas.

The white **OṂ**, born from the self-display of the five wisdoms of the noble ones, is the syllable of combined qualities and is of the nature of the perfection[38] of meditation.[39] It purifies the mental affliction of pride, along with all the results thereby produced—in particular, the suffering of the gods: death and falling. Inseparable from the body and activity of **Shatakratu**,[40] buddha among the gods, it is the self-radiance of the wisdom of equality, arisen in visible form. It guides the six classes of beings to the southern pure realm, The Glorious, and enables them to attain the body of the buddha Ratnasambhava.

The green **MA**, born from the display of the compassionate noble ones' limitless loving-kindness toward all beings, is the syllable of activity and is of the nature of the perfection of patience.[41] It purifies the mental affliction of jealousy, along with all the results thereby produced—in particular, the suffering of the jealous gods: fighting and struggle. Inseparable from the body and activity of **Vemachitra**,[42] buddha among the jealous gods, it is the self-radiance of all-accomplishing wisdom, arisen in visible form. It guides the six classes of beings to the northern pure realm, Perfect Action, and enables them to attain the body of the buddha Amoghasiddhi.

The yellow **ṆI**, born from the display of the great all-pervading and effortless compassion of the noble ones, is the syllable that reverses saṃsāra into the expanse of nirvāṇa on the spot, the vajra wisdom of combined body, speech, mind, and activity. It is of the nature of the perfection of ethics.[43] It purifies the stains of ignorant dualistic fixation, along with all the results thereby produced—in particular, the four great rivers of human suffering: birth, aging, sickness, and death. Inseparable from the body and activity of **Shākyamuni**,[44] the buddha among humans, it is the self-radiance of self-existing wisdom, arisen in visible form. It guides the six classes of beings to the pure realm of Akaniṣhṭha, the completely pure dharmadhātu, and enables them to attain the body of the sixth buddha, Vajradhara.

38. Skt. pāramitā, Tib. *pha rol tu phyin pa*/"*pha-rol tu chin-pa*"
39. Skt. dhyāna, Tib. *bsam gtan*/"*samten*"
40. Tib. *thub pa brgya 'byin*/"*Thubpa Gyajin*," "Performer of a Hundred Sacrifices"
41. Skt. kṣhānti, Tib. *bzod pa*/"*zöpa*"
42. Tib. *thag bzang ris*/"*Thakzang Ri*," "He Who Wears a Brilliant Garment"
43. Skt. shīla, Tib. *tshul khrims*/"*tsultrim*"
44. Tib. *sh'a kya thub pa*/"*Shakya Thubpa*," "Sage of the Shākya [clan]"

The sky blue **PAD**, born from the self-display of limitless equanimity, the compassion of the noble ones that does not lapse into partiality, is the syllable of body and is of the nature of the perfection of supreme knowledge.[45] It purifies the mental affliction of ignorance, along with all the results thereby produced—in particular, the suffering of animals: stupidity, dullness, and servitude. Inseparable from the body and activity of **Dhruvasiṃha**,[46] buddha among the animals, it is the self-radiance of dharmadhātu wisdom, arisen in visible form. It guides the six classes of beings to the central pure realm, The Densely Arrayed, and enables them to attain the body of the buddha Vairochana.

The red **ME**, born from the self-display of limitless joy, the compassion of the noble ones that is equal for all, is the syllable of speech and is of the nature of the perfection of generosity. It purifies attachment and miserliness, along with all the results thereby produced—in particular, the suffering of the hungry ghosts: hunger and thirst. Inseparable from the body and activity of **Jvalamukha**,[47] buddha among the hungry ghosts, it is the self-radiance of discriminating awareness wisdom, arisen in visible form. It guides the six classes of beings to the western pure realm, Sukhāvatī, and enables them to attain the body of the buddha Amitābha.

The black **HŪṂ**, born from the self-display of limitless compassion, the compassion with which the noble ones look upon all beings as they would their own children, is the syllable of mind and is of the nature of the perfection of supreme knowledge. It purifies dualistic anger, along with all the results thereby produced—in particular, the sufferings of hell beings: extreme heat and cold. Inseparable from the body and activity of **Dharmarāja**,[48] buddha among the hell beings, it is the self-radiance of mirror-like wisdom, arisen in visible form. It guides the six classes of beings to the pure realm of True Joy, and enables them to attain the body of the buddha Akṣhobhya. The embodiment of all the energy of the limitless activity of shaking the six classes of beings from the depths of saṃsāra is this very six-syllable king of mantras. Recite it for as long as you are able as the main body of the session.

Finally, the entire phenomenal world, now transformed into kāyas and pure realms by the light from the guru's body on the crown of your head, melts into light and dissolves into guru Avalokita, who in turn melts into light and dissolves into you, after which you too melt into light.

Rest evenly for as long as possible in the luminous emptiness free of any conception about the three spheres[49] that clings to self and other, the deity and mantra. Let go of all references toward fabricated attributes such as existence and nonexistence, "it is" and "it is not," and emptiness or non-emptiness. Free of viewer and viewed, not differentiating appearance, sound, and awareness from emptiness, rest for as long as possible in the mind of the Noble One, the natural face of great all-pervading dharmadhātu.

45. Skt. prajñā, Tib. *shes rab*/"*sherab*"
46. Tib. *seng ge rab brtan*/"*Senge Rabten*," "Steadfast Lion"
47. Tib. *kha la me 'bar*/"*Khala Mebar*," "Mouth of Blazing Flame"
48. Tib. *chos kyi rgyalpo*/"*Chökyi Gyalpo*," "King of Dharma"
49. The "three spheres" are the actor, the action itself, and the object toward which the action is directed.

3.1. Implementing the practice in daily life

When you arise from that, rest evenly in the awareness that everything included in the domain of the five elements—all things that appear as self and other: rocks, mountains, cliffs, and so on—is the body of the Noble Great Compassionate One. All sounds—whether they are conjoined with the life force faculty of sentient beings or, as the sounds of the elements, not so conjoined—are the speech of the Noble One, the melodic resonance of the six syllables. All thoughts are the mind of the Noble One—awareness and emptiness, free of fabrication, the innate character of the dharmakāya. In all activities—walking, sleeping, sitting, or talking—abandon mundane, attached ways of thinking. Being certain about the samādhi of these three outlooks, recite:

> The physical appearance of myself and others is the body of the Noble One.
> Sounds are the melody of the six syllables.
> Thoughts are the expanse of great wisdom.

3.2. Dedicating the roots of virtue to Enlightenment and Making Aspirations

"By the unsurpassable meritorious accumulation of whatever virtue exists in my mindstream, dedicated equally to all sentient beings and symbolized by this meditation and recitation, may I quickly attain the unsurpassable state equal to that of Avalokiteshvara and thereby attain the power that will enable me to establish beings limitless as space, without even a single one left behind, in the state of the noble, supreme Great Compassionate One, inseparable from perfect, genuine enlightenment." Thinking this, recite:

> By this merit, may we quickly
> Accomplish Avalokiteshvara
> And establish all beings without exception
> In that state.

In addition, engage in as many pure-hearted aspirations as you can.

Those who do not have time to practice as described as above should practice as follows.

Start with refuge and bodhichitta as described above. For the main practice, make several supplications with a focused, one-pointed mind, thinking that noble and supreme Avalokita, with all of the appropriate objects of visualization, is seated on the crown of your head, and call to guru Avalokita, thinking, "Consider me!"

Now, OṂ is the syllable of the wisdom of the five kāyas, MAṆI means "jewel," and PADME means "with lotus." Therefore, "Jewel Holder of the Lotus" is an epithet of noble Avalokita. HŪṂ represents his performing the activity of protecting the six classes of beings from suffering. Thus, with a mind of supplication, think, "Embodiment of the five kāyas and five wisdoms, Jewel Holder of the Lotus, please protect the six classes of beings from suffering," while reciting the six syllables as many times as you can.

Finally, the guru Avalokita on the crown of your head, thoroughly pleased, melts into light and dissolves into you.

Think that the wisdom of the Noble One has entered your mindstream and be free of doubt. Through dedicating and making aspirations afterwards, one is sure to attain the benefits listed below. Therefore, all should practice with devotion and joy!

4. The teaching on the benefits

Now I shall speak very briefly on the essence of the immeasurable benefits of practicing the meditation and recitation of noble Avalokita. In regard to meditating on his body or engaging it mentally, the *Root Tantra of the Lotus Net*[47] says:

> The maṇḍala of body that accomplishes meditating
> On all buddhas combined
> Is the body of the protector Avalokita.
> Through meditating on or even recalling it,
> The actions of immediate retribution and all obscurations are purified.

Also, in regard to the benefits of reciting the six syllables, king of secret mantras, here is the stainless speech of the Victorious One, the perfect Buddha Shākyamuni, the parting words left behind by mahāguru Padmākara to the subjects of Tibet, and the treasure-teaching of the great, undisputed, emanated treasure-revealer, vidyādhara Jatsön Nyingpo:

> OṂ MAṆI PADME HŪṂ༔
>
> This six-syllable mantra is the very embodiment of the wisdom heart of all buddhas, the essence of the five buddha families, and the essence of the holders of the secret.༔ It contains the condensed oral instruction of each of the six syllables and is the source of all sugatas and excellent qualities.༔ It is the root of all siddhis that bring benefit and happiness, the great path to the higher realms and liberation.༔ Through even hearing once these six syllables, the supreme speech that is the essence of all dharmas, one attains the level of a non-returner and becomes a liberator and guide of beings.༔ Through hearing it at the time of death, ants and other animals will be freed from that body and born in Sukhāvatī.༔ Through the mere recollection of the six syllables, like the sunrise shining on the snow, all of the misdeeds and obscurations of negative karma that have been accumulated during one's lives in saṃsāra since beginningless time will be purified, and one will be born in Sukhāvatī.༔ Through even touching it, one obtains the empowerments of limit-

47. Tib. *padma dra ba'i rtsa rgyud*/"*pema draway tsagyü*"

less buddhas and bodhisattvas.༔ Meditating on it even once fulfills the objectives of hearing, contemplating, and meditating.༔ All appearances will arise as the dharmakāya, and the treasury of the activity that benefits beings will be opened.༔

Also,

O child of noble family, though it is possible to measure the weight of Mount Meru, king of mountains, in ounces, one cannot measure the merit of reciting once the six syllables.༔ Even if one wipes a cliff of diamonds with kashika cloth only once every hundred years, one will be able to cause its full erosion.༔ Still one cannot measure the merit of reciting once the six syllables.༔ Though one may drain a great ocean one drop at a time, the merit of reciting the six syllables once cannot be exhausted.༔ All the atoms of earth in the whole Land of Snows, and each and every leaf in a verdant forest, can be counted, but the measure of the merit of reciting the six syllables once cannot be taken.༔

Similarly, it is possible to empty a house one hundred miles long filled with sesame seeds, even if one tosses them out one at a time, but the merit of reciting the six syllables once cannot be measured.༔ It is possible to count the number of raindrops that fall in a year, but the merit of reciting the six syllables once cannot be counted.༔ Therefore, child of noble family, it is not necessary for me to continue explaining day and night.༔ For though it is possible to measure the merit of serving ten million tathāgatas like myself, the merit of reciting the six syllables once cannot be measured.༔

This is what closes the gates of birth for the six classes of beings.༔ This is what brings one through the paths and levels of the six perfections.༔ This is what purifies the stains of karma, mental afflictions, and habitual tendencies.༔ This is what refines appearances into the pure realms of the three kāyas.༔

Listen, O children of noble family!༔
This essence, the heart༔
Of the blessings of all victorious ones,༔
Is the source of all benefit and happiness,༔
And the root of all siddhis.༔
It is the ladder that leads to the higher realms.༔
It is the door that blocks the lower realms.༔
It is the ship in which one crosses over saṃsāra.༔

It is the torch that dispels darkness.༔
It is the warrior that conquers the five poisons.༔
It is the blazing fire that burns away misdeeds
  and obscurations.༔
It is the hammer that pounds down suffering.༔
It is the remedy that tames uncultured lands.༔
It is the dharma inheritance of the Land of Snows.༔
It is the condensed, pithy essence༔
Of the many sūtras, tantras, and treatises,༔
And of all hearing, contemplating, and meditating.༔
It is the precious king of mantras.༔
Recite these six syllables!༔

Thus the benefits, which cannot be done justice by words, have been lauded in both the direct oral lineage and the treasure teachings.[48] Since reciting the enlightened speech of the six syllables even once is sure to produce the benefits explained here, do not let your three gates lapse into their mundane states. Make a commitment toward reciting this mantra between one hundred and ten thousand times a day, continuously and without fail, which will gather a vast accumulation of virtue that brings great benefit with little difficulty. Strive in every way to make your life meaningful.

May the rope of the Noble One's compassion
Draw beings up from the ocean of saṃsāra.
May they be confirmed on the mountain of Potala,
The completely free and blissful grove of liberation.

48. Tib. *bka' ma* and *gter ma*/"*kama*" and "*terma*"

A long time had passed after two women, dharma practitioners of noble family, Kelsang Drölkar and her mother Tseten Drölkar, first requested this composition. Later, in response to their repeated requests and as promised, it was composed in a manner that can be easily understood by old householders of low intelligence like myself. Thus it has been written by the hand of someone who in these bad times pretends in name to be a bodhisattva, a beggar made to look like a dharma practitioner, Lodrö Ziji, the sickly old man otherwise called by the name Khakhyab Dorje. May virtue and goodness increase.

The Praise to Avalokiteshvara

by Chandrakīrti

The Praise to Avalokiteshvara
by Chandrakīrti

In the language of India: *Mahākāruṇikakubākyastohrādhiṣhṭana*
In the language of Tibet [translated into English]: **The Lamenting Praise, Endowed with Blessings, to the Great Compassionate One**

I prostrate to the bodhisattva Avalokiteshvara.

Great Compassionate One, noble Avalokita,
Unsurpassed in form, with the color of a stainless conch,
You beautify the center of a pure and luminous disc
of moonlight,
Like the blazing light of a thousand shining suns.

Hero radiating immeasurable luminosity,
Teacher renowned as the guide of the three levels of existence,
Only friend of all beings in the three realms,
Loving protector, compassionate deity, please think of me.

I, since beginningless and endless time,
Have been lost in wrong paths, wandering in saṃsāric existence.
I confess the wrong and harmful actions
I have committed before;
I am remorseful of whatever wrongs I have done.

Due to the incredible power of such karma,
I have sunken in the ocean of saṃsāra's suffering.
The blazing fires of aggression have burnt my mindstream;
The darkness of ignorance has clouded my intelligence.

My consciousness sinks down in the ocean of desire;
I am suppressed in the lower realms by the mountain of pride;
Distracted in saṃsāra by the hurricanes of jealousy,
I am tightly bound up by the knots of self-centricity.

I have fallen into the pit of desire filled with molten stone,
The mud of fierce suffering falls down like rain.
The fire from the blazing sun burns from above,
The water that moistens the earth sends chills from below.

The powerful breeze outside is hot from all sides,
The wind that disturbs everything arises from within.
Even though this suffering is extremely difficult to bear,
How could I renounce the deity to whom I am committed?

Thus I vie against this suffering to maintain my commitments,
And out of devoted faith, I do not abandon you.
So noble protector, what are you thinking in not helping beings?
Caring protector, why do you not love me?

I and others like me are ignorant fools inclined to misdeeds.
Through the power of my karma I was born in this dark age.
I regret this and am so tired of karma,
But even though so disenchanted,
I cannot avert my karma's momentum.

The force of karma is like the flow of a river.
How is one to immediately turn it around?
Though I have entered the teachings, I am unable to abide by them.
My body, speech, and mind have been overpowered by misdeeds.
My consciousnesses, the offspring of the senses,

Are agonized by the fierce and powerful fire
of negative actions.
If this illusory body of aggregates cannot endure this,
Compassionate, loving lord, can you?

Your compassionate face blazes with the light of the sun
And the radiance of the moon.
Though I strive to see it,
My eyes are blinded by the cataracts
of beginningless ignorance.

Protector of beings, where are you now?
Utterly terrified, I shiver with fear.
Wailing with this sad lament,
I cry out to you in desperation.
Loving, compassionate protector, do you hear me?

One day, at the time of death, when my mind and body
part ways,
I will leave my friends and be led away by the lord of death,
Unaccompanied by any close ones from this world.

Through the power of karma, I and those like me
will wander alone.
If at that time I am without any refuge,
Loving protector, will you let me go back into saṃsāra?

NAMA ĀRYAPALO
Those like me who are tormented by karma
Have been mistaken about the way things are
since beginningless time.
With no liberation from saṃsāra's three realms,
The cycle continues through countless births.

The bodies I have taken on are beyond number;
Their flesh and bone amassed together would be
as vast as this world.
Their pus and blood would fill the vastest ocean.
The karma they have gathered is beyond imagination.
Though my births and deaths in saṃsāra's three realms
have been uninterrupted,
Everything I do has been meaningless and wasted.
If from among these limitless births,
In only one I applied myself to the unsurpassable goal
of enlightenment,
This alone would amount to meaningful action.

Yet alas, the force of karma
is strong and mental afflictions are powerful.
I continue to wander along in saṃsāra,
taking on bodies of flesh and blood,
Trapped in the prison of the fierce sufferings of existence.

All of these frightening forms of suffering
Have come about due to the karma of my negative actions.
Therefore, Great Compassionate One,
Please reverse this wind of afflicted karma!

Since this karmic wind is so strong,
And could cause me to wander forever
in the darkness of ignorance,
Won't you look upon me with the brilliant rays
of your torch-like wisdom?
Since these results of negative actions
are so unbearable,
Great Compassionate One, won't you help me
with your Buddha activity?

Since I am tortured by the unbearable illness
of the three poisons,
Won't you heal me with the medicine of your compassionate
skillful means?
Since I have fallen into the gorge of wrong views,
Compassionate One, won't you quickly pull me up
with your hand?
Since the fire of fierce suffering's strong karma is blazing,
Won't you send down the cooling rain of your compassion?

For if I languish in the three realms of saṃsāra
Letting my karmic results erode the actions that caused them,
Compassionate One, what need will there be to call on you?
If you allow sentient beings to exhaust their own karma,
Noble One, of what use is your compassion?

Supreme One, if you truly possess the power of compassion,
Do not be idle, lazy, and indifferent.
I call to you from my heart—look upon us,
O compassionate, victorious deity!

Thus ends The Lamenting Praise, Endowed with Blessings, to the Great Compassionate One, *composed by Chandrakīrti, a master of the five fields of learning.*

The Thirty-Seven Practices of Bodhisattvas

by Ngulchu Thogme

The Thirty-Seven Practices of Bodhisattvas

Namo Lokeshvaraya

Though you see all phenomena as free of coming and going
You strive only for the benefit of beings.
To the supreme guru and the protector Avalokita,
I always bow with respect in my three gates. (A)

Perfect buddhas, the source of all benefit and happiness,
Arise through accomplishing the genuine dharma.
Since this in turn depends on knowing the practices,
The practices of bodhisattvas will here be explained. (B)

Having now attained the great vessel of freedoms and resources, so difficult to find,
In order to bring oneself and others across the ocean of saṃsāra,
Day and night without break
To listen, reflect, and meditate is the practice of bodhisattvas. (1)

Attachment towards friends churns like water.
Hatred towards enemies burns like fire.
Dark with ignorance that forgets what to adopt or reject—
To give up one's homeland is the practice of bodhisattvas. (2)

Free from negative places, mental afflictions gradually decrease.
With no distractions, virtuous activity naturally grows.
Through clear intelligence, certainty in the dharma is born—
To rely on places of solitude is the practice of bodhisattvas. (3)

One will part with each of one's familiar friends and relatives
And leave behind the wealth one strived to gain.
Consciousness, the guest, will leave the guesthouse of the body behind—
To let go of this life is the practice of bodhisattvas. (4)

Make friends with this one and the three poisons grow,
The activities of listening, reflecting, and meditating decline,
And lovingkindness and compassion are destroyed.
To cast off bad friends is the practice of bodhisattvas. (5)

Rely on this one and defects disappear,
While qualities increase like the light of the waxing moon.
To cherish such a genuine spiritual friend
More dearly than one's own body is the practice of bodhisattvas. (6)

Bound themselves in the prison of saṃsāra,
Who can worldly gods protect?
Therefore, in seeking undeceiving protection, to go for refuge
To the three jewels is the practice of bodhisattvas. (7)

Sufferings of the lower realms, so very difficult to bear,
Result from misdeeds, so taught the Sage.
Therefore, even at the risk of one's life,
To never commit misdeeds is the practice of bodhisattvas. (8)

Happiness of the three realms is like dew on a blade of grass:
Its very nature is to quickly disappear.
To strive for the supreme state of liberation,
Which never changes, is the practice of bodhisattvas. (9)

From beginningless time my mothers have cared for me;
If they suffer, what good is my own happiness?
Therefore, in order to liberate limitless sentient beings,
To engender bodhichitta is the practice of bodhisattvas. (10)

All suffering comes from wanting happiness for oneself,
Perfect buddhas are born from the wish to benefit others.
Therefore, to genuinely exchange one's happiness
For the suffering of others is the practice of bodhisattvas. (11)

Even if someone, out of great desire, steals all my wealth
Or makes another do so,
To dedicate body, possessions, and all virtue of the three times
To them is the practice of bodhisattvas. (12)

Even if someone were to sever my head
Though I had not done the slightest wrong,
To still take on their misdeeds
With compassion is the practice of bodhisattvas. (13)

Although someone broadcasts throughout the triple universe
A legion of unpleasant things about me,
In return, with a mind full of lovingkindness,
To tell of their qualities is the practice of bodhisattvas. (14)

Although in a gathering of many people
Someone uses harsh words and reveals my hidden faults,
Seeing them as a spiritual friend,
To bow with respect is the practice of bodhisattvas. (15)

Even if someone who I cared for as my child
Were to view me as an enemy,
Like a mother would her ailing child,
To love them even more is the practice of bodhisattvas. (16)

Although someone, my equal or less,
Through pride sought to put me down,
With respect as for a guru,
To place them above my head is the practice of bodhisattvas. (17)

Though immersed in poverty and always scorned by others,
Plagued by grave illness and evil spirits too,
To take on still the misdeeds and suffering of all beings
Without losing heart is the practice of bodhisattvas. (18)

Though famed and bowed to by many beings,
And affluent as a god of wealth,
To see as insubstantial the prosperity of existence,
And thus be free of arrogance, is the practice of bodhisattvas. (19)

Without conquering the enemy of one's own aggression,
Trying to conquer outer enemies will only cause them to spread.
Therefore, with the army of lovingkindness and compassion,
To tame one's mindstream is the practice of bodhisattvas. (20)

The sense pleasures are just like salt water:
However much one consumes, craving only increases.
To immediately discard things
That give rise to attachment is the practice of bodhisattvas. (21)

However they appear, all appearances are one's mind.
Mind in itself is primordially free of elaborations' extremes.
Knowing this, to not mentally engage the attributes
Of subject and object is the practice of bodhisattvas. (22)

When meeting with an attractive object,
Treat it as a rainbow in summer:
A beautiful appearance, but not viewed as real—
To give up attachment is the practice of bodhisattvas. (23)

All varieties of suffering are like the death of one's child in a dream:
Taking mistaken appearances to be real—how exhausting!
Therefore, when encountering difficult situations,
To see them as confusion is the practice of bodhisattvas. (24)

If those aspiring to enlightenment must give even their body,
What need to mention outer objects?
Therefore, without hope of return or ripened results,
To extend generosity is the practice of bodhisattvas. (25)

If without discipline one cannot even benefit oneself,
What a laugh to think of helping others!
Therefore, free of worldly craving,
To maintain discipline is the practice of bodhisattvas. (26)

For bodhisattvas desiring the wealth of virtue,
Anything that harms is like a treasury of jewels.
Therefore, free of aggression towards anyone,
To cultivate patience is the practice of bodhisattvas. (27)

If hearers and solitary realizers, for their benefit alone,
Practice diligence like their heads are on fire,
Then certainly, for the good of all beings, to apply diligence,
The source of good qualities, is the practice of bodhisattvas. (28)

Knowing that vipashyanā fully endowed with shamatha
Vanquishes the mental afflictions,
To engage in concentration that correctly transcends
The four formless ones is the practice of bodhisattvas. (29)

Without supreme knowledge, five perfections
Will not result in perfect enlightenment.
Therefore, to cultivate supreme knowledge, endowed with skillful means
And free of conceptions of the three spheres, is the practice of bodhisattvas. (30)

If one does not examine one's own confusion,
It is possible to act non-dharmically with the guise of a practitioner.
Therefore, to continually examine
And abandon one's confusion is the practice of bodhisattvas. (31)

If, governed by mental afflictions, one speaks of the faults of other bodhisattvas,
Oneself will be diminished.
Therefore, to not speak of the faults of those
Who have entered the Mahāyāna path is the practice of bodhisattvas. (32)

Through desire for honor and gain, disputes arise
And the activities of hearing, contemplating, and meditating decline.
Therefore, to give up attachment to the households
Of friends, relatives, and donors is the practice of bodhisattvas. (33)

Harsh speech disturbs the minds of others,
And weakens the conduct of bodhisattvas.
Therefore, to abandon harsh speech,
Unpleasant to the minds of others, is the practice of bodhisattvas. (34)

As mental afflictions of habit are difficult to counter with remedies,
The one with mindfulness and attentiveness takes up the weapon of the antidote,
And slays mental afflictions like desire
The moment they arise—such is the practice of bodhisattvas. (35)

In sum, wherever you are and whatever you do,
Always remaining mindful and attentive
To the state of your mind,
To accomplish the benefit of others is the practice of bodhisattvas. (36)

Taking up the virtue so diligently gathered in this way,
So that the suffering of limitless beings may be dispelled,
And with the wisdom of threefold purity,
To dedicate it to enlightenment is the practice of bodhisattvas. (37)

Following the contents of the sūtras and treatises
And the teachings of genuine masters,
I have written these thirtyseven practices of bodhisattvas
For the sake of those who wish to train in the bodhisattva path. [C]

Since my intelligence is low and the sum of my training small,
I cannot offer verse that is pleasing to the scholars.
Yet since they are based on the sūtras and the teachings of genuine masters,
I believe these bodhisattva practices are free of error. [D]

Yet alas, as the depth of the vast deeds of bodhisattvas
Is hard to fathom by limited minds like mine,
I request the forgiveness of the holy ones
For all errors of contradiction, omission, and so on. [E]

By the virtue arising from this,
May all beings, through ultimate and relative bodhichitta,
Not dwelling in the extremes of peace or existence,
Be equal to the protector Avalokita. [F]

For the benefit of self and other, this was written by Thogme, a monk who follows scripture and reasoning, at the Ngulchu Rinchen Cave.

PART TWO:
The Tibetan Texts

༄༅།། གྲུབ་པའི་དབང་ཕྱུག་ལྕགས་ཟམ་པ་ཆེན་པོའི་ཉེ་བརྒྱུད་ཡི་གེ་དྲུག་པའི་སྒོམ་ལུང་འབོག་
ཚུལ་གཞན་ཕན་མཁའ་ཁྱབ་ཅེས་བྱ་བ་བཞུགས་སོ། །

THE TIBETAN TEXT:

The Benefit of Others That Fills All of Space

by **Jamgon Kongtrul**

༄༅། །གྲུབ་པའི་དབང་ཕྱུག་ལྕགས་ཟམ་པ་ཆེན་པོའི་ཉེ་བརྒྱུད་ཡི་གེ་དྲུག་པའི་སྒོམ་ལུང་འབོག་ཚུལ་གཞན་ཕན་མཁའ་ཁྱབ་ཅེས་བྱ་བ་བཞུགས་སོ། །

ན་མོ་ལོ་ཀེ་ཤྭ་ར་ཡ།།
སྙིགས་འགྲོ་ཉམ་ཐག་སྐྱོང་བའི་ཡབ།།
འཇིག་རྟེན་དབང་ཕྱུག་བརྩོན་འགྲུས་མཚན།།
གང་གི་གདམས་པའི་མཛོད་འཛིན་པ།།
འགྲོ་མགོན་བླ་མར་ཕྱག་བྱས་ནས།།
སྤྱན་རས་གཟིགས་དབང་ཞལ་གྱི་ལུང་།།
གྲུབ་ཐོབ་ཆེན་པོའི་ཁྱད་པར་ཆོས།།
འཁོར་བ་དོང་སྤྲུགས་གདམས་ངག་བཅུད།།
ཆོས་སྒོ་བརྒྱད་ཁྲིའི་སྙིང་པོ་འཆད།།

འདིར་འབྲེལ་ཚད་དོན་ལྡན་གྱི་བཟང་པོ་སྤྱོད་ལ་ཞུགས་པའི་དགེ་བའི་བཤེས་གཉེན་དག་གིས་སྐལ་པ་མཆོག་དམན་མ་བརྟགས་པར་ཐོས་པ་ཙམ་གྱིས་ཕན་ཡོན་སྙིང་ལ་བཞགས་ནས། རེ་བ་དང་ཟང་ཟིང་མེད་པའི་ཆོས་སྦྱིན་སྤུལ་བར་འདོད་པས། འདུས་པའི་དབུས་སུ་སེམས་བསྐྱེད་བཟང་པོ་དང་ལྡན་པས་ཆོས་ཀྱི་ཁྲི་ལ་འཁོད། གྲུབ་ན་རང་ཉིད་ཀྱིས་སྒོམ་བཟླས་མདོར་བསྡུས་བྱས་རྗེས། དེ་འདི་སྐད་ཅེས། ཀྭ། མ་གྱུར་ནམ་མཁའ་དང་མཉམ་པའི་སེམས་ཅན་ཐམས་ཅད་ཡང་དག་པར་རྫོགས་པའི་སངས་རྒྱས་ཀྱི་གོ་འཕང་འཐོབ་པར་བྱ། དེའི་ཆེད་དུ་ཡི་གེ་དྲུག་པའི་བསྒོམ་ལུང་ཟབ་མོ་གསན་ལ། དོན་ཚུལ་བཞིན་དུ་ཉམས་སུ་ལེན་པར་བགྱིའོ་སྙམ་པའི་ཐུགས་བསྐྱེད་རྣམ་པར་དག་པ་དང་ལྡན་པའི་ངང་ནས། ས་ཕྱོགས་འདི་ཉིད་དག་པའི་ཞིང་ཁམས་བདེ་བ་ཅན། སློབ་དཔོན་ཡང་འཕགས་པ་སྤྱན་རས་གཟིགས་དངོས་ཡིན་སྙམ་པའི་འདུ་ཤེས་དང་ལྡན་པས། ལུས་ཀྱིས་ཐལ་སྦྱར་སོགས་གུས་པའི་ཚུལ། ངག་གི་ཙ་ཅོ་སྤངས་ཤིང་སེམས

གཞན་དུ་མི་གཡེངས་པར་མཉན་བྱ་དམ་པའི་ཆོས་དང་། དེ་སྟོན་བྱེད་དགེ་བའི་བཤེས་གཉེན་ལ་གུས་པ་རྩེ་གཅིག་པས་གསན་པར་ཞུ། དེའང་འཕགས་མཆོག་སྤྱན་རས་གཟིགས་དང་པདྨ་འབྱུང་གནས་དབྱེར་མེད་རྣལ་འབྱོར་བརྟུལ་ཞུགས་སྤྱོད་པའི་སྐུར་བསྟན་པ་གྲུབ་པའི་དབང་ཕྱུག་ཐང་སྟོང་རྒྱལ་པོ་ཞེས་མཚན་ཉི་ཟླ་ལྟར་གྲགས་པ་དེ་ཉིད། སྐུ་གཞོན་ནུའི་ཚེ་ཡིག་དྲུག་དུང་ཕྱུར་གྱི་ཚོགས་དཔོན་མཛད་པའི་དུས་ན། ཆོ་འཕྲུལ་ཟླ་བའི་ཚེས་བརྒྱད་ཀྱི་ཐོ་རངས་ཀྱི་ཚེ་ལ། སྐུ་མདུན་གྱི་བུམ་པའི་ཁ་རྒྱན་དེ། དཔག་བསམ་གྱི་སྡོང་པོ་ཆེན་པོར་གྱུར་པའི་ཡལ་འདབ་ཀྱི་ཁྲོད་དུ་པད་ཟླའི་གདན་བཞི་བརྩེགས་པའི་འོག་ནས་ཡར་རིམ་བཞིན་འཕགས་པ་སྤྱན་རས་གཟིགས། ཁ་སརྤ་ཎི། ཛ་ཕྱག་བཞི་པ། བརྒྱད་པ། ཕྱག་སྟོང་སྤྱན་སྟོང་གི་སྐུ་མཚན་དཔེས་བརྒྱན་པ་འོད་ཀྱི་དཀྱིལ་འཁོར་གྱི་དབུས་ན་བཞེངས་སྟབས་སུ་བཞུགས་པའི་མཐའ་བསྐོར་དུ། རྟ་མགྲིན། བདུད་རྩི་འཁྱིལ་པ། སྒྲོལ་མ། རྣམ་པར་རྒྱལ་མ། ཕྱོགས་བཅུའི་སངས་རྒྱས་རྣམས་ཀྱིས་བསྐོར་བ། འོག་གི་ཆ་ལ་ཕྱོགས་སྐྱོང་བཅུ་དང་། གནོད་སྦྱིན་བཅུ་གཉིས། རྒྱལ་ཆེན་བཞིས་བསྐོར་བ་མངོན་སུམ་དུ་གཟིགས་པས། ཡན་ལག་བདུན་པའི་མཆོད་པ་དང་གསོལ་འདེབས་མཛད་པས། རིགས་ཀྱི་བུ་ཁྱོད་ནམ་བྱང་ཆུབ་མ་ཐོབ་ཀྱི་བར་དུ་དགེ་བའི་བཤེས་གཉེན་ང་ཡིན་པས། ཡི་གེ་དྲུག་པའི་སྒོ་ནས་ཕྲིན་ལས་རྒྱ་ཆེན་པོ་བསྒྲུབ་ཅིང་། འགྲོ་བ་རྣམས་འདྲེན་པར་གྱིས་ཤིག །ཅེས་དང་གདམས་པ་མང་དུ་གསུངས་ཤིང་། གཞན་ཡང་ལན་དུ་མར་ཞལ་དངོས་སུ་བསྟན་ནས་སྩལ་བའི་གདམས་པའི་སྙིང་པོ། ཟབ་ལ་བདེ་བ་ཡི་གེ་དྲུག་པའི་སྒོམ་བཟླས་ཀྱི་ལུང་འབོགས་ཤིང་ཉམས་སུ་ལེན་པར་བྱེད་པ་ལ་གསུམ།

སྔོན་འགྲོ་སྐྱབས་སེམས་དང་ལྡན་པས་བློ་ཆོས་ལ་བསྐུལ་བ། དངོས་གཞི་མཁའ་ཁྱབ་ཀྱི་ཏིང་ངེ་འཛིན་དང་འབྲེལ་བར་བསྐྱེད་བཟླས་རྫོགས་གསུམ་བྱ་བ། རྗེས་ལམ་ཁྱེར་གསུམ་དང་ལྡན་པས་དགེ་རྩ་གཞན་དོན་དུ་བསྔོ་བའོ།

དང་པོ་ནི། །རང་ཉིད་གང་དུ་གནས་པའི་མདུན་གྱི་ནམ་མཁར་རིན་པོ་ཆེའི་ཁྲི་དང་པད་ཟླའི་གདན་ལ། ངོ་བོ་རྩ་བའི་བླ་མ་ཉིད་རྣམ་པ་སྤྱན་རས་གཟིགས་འགྲོ་འདུལ་ཕྱག་བཞི་པའི་སྐུར་གསལ་བའི་འཁོར་དུ་སངས་རྒྱས་བྱང་སེམས་དཔག་ཏུ་མེད་པས་བསྐོར་ཏེ་བཞུགས་པའི་མདུན་དུ། བདག་གཞན་སེམས་ཅན་ཐམས་ཅད་དུས་འདི་ནས་བཟུང་རྫོགས་པའི་བྱང་ཆུབ་མ་ཐོབ་ཀྱི་བར་དུ་སྙིང་ཐག་པ་ནས་སྐྱབས་སུ་འགྲོ་སྙམ་པའི་བློ་རྩེ་གཅིག་པས་སྐྱབས་འགྲོའི་ཚིག་ལུགས་ཟབ་པའི་ཐུན་མོང་མ་ཡིན་པའི་སྐྱབས་འགྲོ་དཀྱུ་སྐོར་དུ་གྲགས་པ་ཐུགས་རྗེ་ཆེན་པོས་ཀ་ལྷ་པ་དཔལ་འབྱོར་ཤེས་རབ་ལ་གསུངས་ནས་གྲུབ་ཆེན་ལ་གནང་བར་བཀའ་བསྒོས་པ་ལྟར་བསྐུལ་བའི་བྱིན་བརླབས་མྱོང་གྲུབ་ཀྱིས་ཆེ་བ་འདི་ལ་བྱ་སྟེ། གོང་དུ་ཇི་སྐད་བཤད་པ་ལྟར་དམིགས་པ་རྩེ་གཅིག་པས་སྐྱབས་འགྲོའི་ཚིག་འདི་ལྷན་ཅིག་ཏུ་གནང་བར་ཞུ།

མ་ནམ་མཁའ་དང་མཉམ་པའི་སེམས་ཅན་ཐམས་ཅད་བླ་མ་སངས་རྒྱས་རིན་པོ་ཆེ་ལ་སྐྱབས་སུ་མཆིའོ།།

སངས་རྒྱས་ཆོས་དང་དགེ་འདུན་རྣམས་ལ་སྐྱབས་སུ་མཆིའོ།།

བླ་མ་ཡི་དམ་མཁའ་འགྲོའི་ཚོགས་ལ་སྐྱབས་སུ་མཆིའོ།།

རང་སེམས་སྟོང་གསལ་ཆོས་ཀྱི་སྐུ་ལ་སྐྱབས་སུ་མཆིའོ།།

སློམ་ལུང་འབོགས་སྐབས་ཚར་གསུམ་བདུན་གང་རུང་ལྡན་ཅིག་ཏུ་བརྗོད་པའམ་རྗེས་ཟློས་བྱ་སྟེ་འོག་མ་རྣམས་ལའང་ཤེས་པར་བྱའོ།

ཞེས་བརྒྱ་རྩ་ཉེར་གཅིག །བདུན་ལ་སོགས་པ་ཡོངས་ཁྱབ་དང་སྦྱར་ཏེ་བརྗོད་པའི་རྗེས་སུ། སྐྱབས་ཡུལ་འོད་དུ་ཞུ། རང་ལ་ཐིམ་པས་ཐུགས་རྗེའི་བྱིན་རླབས་ཞུགས། བློ་ཆོས་སུ་དང་གིས་འགྲོ་ཞིང་བར་ཆད་མེད་པར་བསམ། དེའི་རྗེས་ཐོབ་ཏུ། ནམ་མཁའ་དང་མཉམ་པའི་ཕ་མ་སེམས་ཅན་ཐམས་ཅད་འཁོར་བ་སྡུག་བསྔལ་གྱི་རྒྱ་མཚོར་དུས་རྟག་ཏུ་འཁྱམས་པ་སྙིང་རེ་རྗེ། འདི་རྣམས་ཐམས་ཅད་བདག་གིས་ནས་རྫོགས་པའི་སངས་རྒྱས་ཀྱི་གོ་འཕང་ལ་འགོད་པར་བྱ། དེའི་ནུས་པ་བདག་ལ་མེད་པས་ཆོས་ཐམས་ཅད་ཀྱི་སྙིང་པོ་ཡི་གེ་དྲུག་པའི་སློམ་བཟླས་ཉམས་སུ་བླངས་ལ་མྱུར་བ་ཉིད་དུ་སེམས་ཅན་རྣམས་དགྲོལ་བར་བྱ་སྙམ་པ་མཉན་པའམ་ཕྱུགས་རྗེ་ལྷ་བུའི་སེམས་བསྐྱེད་དང་ལྡན་པས། ངག་ཏུ་འདི་གསུང་བར་ཞུ།

སེམས་ཅན་ཐམས་ཅད་ཡང་དག་པར་རྫོགས་པའི་སངས་རྒྱས་ཀྱི་གོ་འཕང་ཐོབ་པར་བྱ།

དེའི་ཆེད་དུ་འཕགས་པ་ཐུགས་རྗེ་ཆེན་པོའི་སློམ་བཟླས་ཉམས་སུ་བླང་བར་བགྱིའོ།

ཞེས་གྲངས་སུ་བརྗོད་ཅིང་ལྷག་བསམ་བཟང་པོ་རྒྱུད་ལ་འགྲེ་དེས་བྱ། སྐྱབས་འགྲོ་ཐོག་མར་བྱས་པས་སྡོམ་པ་ཐམས་ཅད་ཀྱི་རྟེན་དུ་འགྱུར། བློ་ཆོས་སུ་འགྲོ། ལམ་སྒྲུབ་པ་ལ་བར་ཆད་མི་འབྱུང་། སེམས་བསྐྱེད་པས་དཔྱིན་ཆད་བསམ་སྦྱོར་ཅི་བྱས་བྱང་ཆུབ་ཀྱི་གྲོགས་སུ་འགྱུར་བས་ཆོས་ལམ་དུ་འགྲོ་བའི་དགོས་པ་ཡོད་དོ།

དེ་ནས་ཁ་ནང་དུ་ལོག་པའི་དྲན་པས་བློ་ཆོས་སུ་བསྒྱུལ་བ་ལ་གསུམ། ངེས་འབྱུང་གི་གཞི་བཏིང་བ། བརྩོན་འགྲུས་ཀྱི་ལྕག་སྐྱོལ་བ། ཕྱུགས་རྗེ་ལྷ་བུའི་སེམས་བསྐྱེད་ཀྱི་མཚམས་སྦྱར་བའོ། དང་པོ་ལ་སྤྱི་དང་བྱེ་བྲག་ཏུ་དབྱེ་པ་གཉིས་ལས།

སྤྱིར་ཐོག་མ་མེད་པ་ནས་བདག་མེད་པ་ལ་བདག་ཏུ་བཟུང་སྟེ་རྒྱུ་མ་རིག་པ། རྐྱེན་ལས་དང་ཉོན་མོངས་པས་བསྐྱེད་པའི་འགྲོ་བ་རིགས་དྲུག་གི་སྣང་

བ་སོ་སོར་སྣང་བ་འདི་རྣམས་ལ་དཔྱད་པས། རྨི་ལམ་གྱི་དགྲ་གཉེན་ནམ་སྒྱུ་མའི་རྒྱལ་སྲིད་ལྟར་རང་ངོས་ནས་བདེན་པར་གྲུབ་པ་རྡུལ་ཕྲ་མོ་ཙམ་མེད་ཀྱང་། འཁྲུལ་སྣང་ལ་བདེན་པར་བཟུང་སྟེ། ཉོན་མོངས་པ་བག་ཉལ་གྱིས་ཁྱབ་པ་འདུ་བྱེད་ཀྱི་སྡུག་བསྔལ། བདེ་བ་ལྟར་སྣང་ཡང་མྱུར་དུ་མི་རྟག་པ་འགྱུར་བའི་སྡུག་བསྔལ། ལས་ངན་པའི་འབྲས་བུ་མངོན་དུ་སྨྱོང་པ་སྡུག་བསྔལ་གྱི་སྡུག་བསྔལ་ཏེ། དཔེར་ན་ཏིལ་ལ་སྣུམ་གྱིས་ཁྱབ་པ་བཞིན་དུ་ཁམས་གསུམ་རིགས་དྲུག་གི་སེམས་ཅན་རྣམས་སྡུག་བསྔལ་ཆེན་པོ་དེ་གསུམ་ལས་མ་འདས་པས་འཁོར་བ་འདིར་བདེ་བ་སྐྲ་རྩེའི་ཆ་ཤས་ཙམ་ཡང་མེད་པ་ལ་བསམས་ཏེ་ངེས་འབྱུང་དྲག་ཏུ་བསྐྱེད། བྱེ་བྲག་རིགས་དྲུག་རེ་རེ་ནས་དཔྱད་དེ། དེའང་མདོ་སྡེ་དྲན་པ་ཉེར་བཞག་ལས།

སེམས་ཅན་དམྱལ་བ་དམྱལ་མེས་ཉམས།།
ཡི་དྭགས་བཀྲེས་ཤིང་སྐོམ་པས་ཉམས།།
དུད་འགྲོ་གཅིག་ལ་གཅིག་ཟས་ཉམས།།
ལྷ་དག་བག་མེད་པ་ཡིས་ཉམས།།
ལྷ་མིན་འཐབ་ཅིང་རྩོད་པས་ཉམས།།
མི་དག་འཚོ་བ་ཐུང་པས་ཉམས།།
འཁོར་བ་ཁབ་ཀྱི་རྩེ་ཙམ་ཡང་།།
བདེ་བ་ནམ་ཡང་ཡོད་མ་ཡིན།།

ཞེས་གསུངས་པ་ལྟར་སྲིད་རྩེ་ནས་མནར་མེད་བར་འཁོར་བའི་གནས་མཐོ་དམན་གང་དུ་སྐྱེས་ཀྱང་སྡུག་བསྔལ་ཁོ་ནའི་རང་བཞིན། དཔེར་ན་དུག་དང་འདྲེས་པའི་ཁ་ཟས་ལ་རྣམ་པ་བཟང་ངན་གྱི་ཁྱད་པར་མེད་པས་སྤང་བར་བྱ་བ་བཞིན་དུ་འཁོར་བ་ལས་ངེས་པར་འབྱུང་བའི་བློ་བརྟན་པོར་བསྐྱེད་པར་བྱའོ།

གཉིས་པ་ནི། དེ་དག་ལས་ཀྱང་ཁྱད་པར་དུ་རང་རེ་མིའི་གནས་སྣང་འདི་ལ་དཔྱད་པས། མི་ཁོམ་པའི་གནས་བརྒྱད་དུ་མ་སྐྱེས་པས་དལ་བ་བརྒྱད། རང་འབྱོར་ལྔ། གཞན་འབྱོར་ལྔ་སྟེ་དལ་འབྱོར་གྱི་ཆོས་བཅོ་བརྒྱད་དང་ལྡན་པའི་མིའི་ལུས་རྙེད་པ་ཤིན་ཏུ་དཀའ་ཞིང་། རྙེད་ན་ཕན་ཐོགས་ཆེ་བས་རིན་པོ་ཆེ་དང་ཆོས་མཚུངས་པས་འདི་ཉིད་རྒྱུ་དང་དཔེ་དང་གྲངས་སོགས་ཀྱི་སྒོ་ནས་ཐོབ་པར་དཀའ་སྟེ། ངན་སོང་གི་འགྲོ་བ་ས་ཆེན་པོའི་རྡུལ་ཙམ་ཡོད་ལ་མི་ལུས་ཙམ་

པོ་པའང་སེན་མོའི་སྙིང་གི་རྟུལ་དང་འདྲ་བར་ཡོད་པ་ལས། ཆོས་ལྡན་གྱི་མི་ལུས་ནི་ཉིན་མོའི་སྐར་མ་ལྟར་དཀོན་ཏེ། སྙིང་རྗེ་པད་དཀར་ལས།

མིར་སྐྱེ་བ་ནི་རྙེད་པར་དཀའ།།
དལ་བ་ཕུན་སུམ་ཚོགས་པའང་རྙེད་པར་དཀའ།།
སངས་རྒྱས་འཇིག་རྟེན་དུ་འབྱུང་བའང་རྙེད་པར་དཀའ།།
དགེ་བའི་ཆོས་ལ་འདུན་པའང་རྙེད་པར་དཀའ།།
ཡང་དག་པའི་སྨོན་ལམ་ཡང་རྙེད་པར་དཀའ་བ་ལགས་སོ།།

ཞེས་སོགས་མཐའ་ཡས་པ་གསུངས་ལ། དེ་ལྟ་བུའི་མི་ལུས་ཐོབ་ཀྱང་སྐྱེ་རྒ་ན་འཆིའི་ཆུ་བོ་ཆེན་པོ་བཞི་ལས་མ་འདས་པས་རྟག་པ་དང་བདེ་བ་སྐྱིད་ཅིག་ཀྱང་མེད། དེའང་སྤྱིར་འདུས་བྱས་ཐམས་ཅད་ཀྱང་མི་རྟག་པའི་མཐའ་བཞིས་དབང་དུ་བྱས་པ་སྟེ་འདུས་པའི་མཐར་འབྲལ། བསགས་པའི་མཐར་འཛད། མཐོ་བའི་མཐར་དམའ། སྐྱེས་པའི་མཐར་ངེས་པར་འཆི། སྐྱོས་མིའི་ལུས་ནམ་འཆིའི་ཆ་མེད་ཅིང་འཆི་རྐྱེན་གང་གིས་ཀྱང་བྱེད་ངེས་པ་མེད། གསོད་སར་ཁྲིད་པའི་བཙོན་བཞིན་ཞག་རེ་སོང་བ་དང་འཆི་བ་ལ་ཧ་ཅང་ཉེར་འགྲོ། ཆུའི་ཆུ་བུར། རི་གཟར་གྱི་ཐབ། ནམ་མཁའི་གློག་ལྟར་གློ་བུར་མྱུར་བ་ཁོ་ནར་འཆི་བ་ཐོག་ཏུ་འོང་། མཁས་བཙུན་བཙན་ཕྱུག་དཔའ་རྩལ་མོ་གཏོ་སྨན་དཔྱད་གང་གིས་ཀྱང་བཟློག་ཏུ་མེད། ལོངས་སྤྱོད་དབང་ཐང་སྙན་གྲགས་གང་ཡང་རྗེས་སུ་མི་འབྲང་བས་དགེ་སྡིག་གི་ལས་ཁོ་ན་རྣམ་པར་ཤེས་པ་དང་འགྲོགས་ནས་ཚེ་ཕྱི་མའི་གནས་སུ་འགྲོ་བའི་ཚེ་སྡིག་པས་ངན་སོང་དུ་ལྟུང་། དགེ་བས་མཐོ་རིས་དང་ཐར་པ་ཐོབ་པ་ཡིན་པས་དེས་ན་ཚེ་ཕྱི་མ་ཕན་ཆད་ལ་ཕན་པ་དམ་པའི་ཆོས་མ་གཏོགས་གཅིག་ཀྱང་མེད། ཚེ་ཕྱི་མ་ལྟ་ཅི་སྨོས། ཚེ་འདི་ལའང་འཕྲལ་ཡུན་གཉིས་ཀར་ཕན་པ་ཆེ་བ་དམ་པའི་ཆོས་ཁོ་ན་ཡིན་ཅིང་། སང་བྱེད་གཞང་བྱེད་ཀྱི་ལོང་སྐབས་མེད་པས་ད་ལྟ་ཉིད་ནས་ལས་འབྲས་ལ་ཡིད་ཆེས་པའི་དད་པ་དང་། བླ་མ་དཀོན་མཆོག་ལ་སེམས་དྭངས་པའི་དད་པ་དང་། བྱང་ཆུབ་བསྒྲུབ་པ་ལ་འདོད་པའི་དད་པ་སྟེ། དེ་གསུམ་དང་ལྡན་པས་ལུས་ལ་གཡོག་དང་གྱ་ཡི་འདུ་ཤེས་བཞག་སྟེ་དམ་པའི་ཆོས་ཁོ་ན་ལ་མི་འབྱུང་རེ་སྐམ་པའི་དམ་བཅའ་བརྟན་པར་བྱའོ།

གསུམ་པ་ནི། ཡང་འདི་སྐམ་དུ་བསམ་སྟེ། ཨ་ཙ་མ། བདག་གིས་མི་ལུས་ཉིན་མོའི་སྐར་བ་དང་འདྲ་བ་ཡུད་ཙམ་པ་འདི་ལ་ལུས་ཀྱི་སྒོ་ནས་ཇི་ལྟར་བཀྱིས་ན་རླབས་པོ་ཆེའི་དགེ་བ་ཞིག་འགྲུབ། ངག་གི་སྒོ་ནས་ཇི་ལྟར་སྨྲས་ན་གཞན་ལ་ཕན་པའི་དགེ་བ་ལ་འབྲུལ། ཡིད་ཀྱི་སྒོ་ནས་ཇི་ལྟར་བསམ་ན་སེམས་ཅན་ཡོངས་ལ་ཁྱབ་པའི་དགེ་བར་འགྱུར་སྙམ་དུ་མདོར་ན་ལུས་ངག་ཡིད་གསུམ་སེམས་ཅན་དོན་དུ་བཀོལ་བའི་ལྷག་བསམ་རྒྱ་ཆེན་པོ་བསྐྱེད། དོན་དེ་དག་འགྲུབ་པའི་ཕྱིར། སངས་རྒྱས་ཐམས་ཅད་ཀྱི་སྙིང་རྗེའི་རང་གཟུགས། བོད་ཁ་བ་ཅན་གྱི་ལྷ་སྐལ། ཛོ་བོ་ཐུགས་རྗེ་ཆེན་པོ་ལ་གསོལ་བ་འདེབས་སོ་སྙམ་པས་མཁའ

ཁྱབ་ཀྱི་དམིགས་པ་ལ་འཇུག་གོ།

གཉིས་པ་དངོས་གཞི་ལ་གསུམ། བསྐྱེད་རིམ་བསྒོམ་པ། བཟླས་པ་བྱ་བ། རྫོགས་རིམ་བསྒོམ་པའོ།

དང་པོ་ནི། །བདག་སོགས་འགྲོ་དྲུག་སེམས་ཅན་ཐམས་ཅད་ཀྱི་སྤྱི་བོའི་གཙུག་ཏུ་པདྨ་དཀར་པོ་དང་ཟླ་བའི་གདན་ལ་ཡི་གེ་ཧྲཱིཿལས་འབྱུངས་པའི་འཕགས་མཆོག་སྤྱན་རས་གཟིགས་དབང་ཕྱུག་སྐུ་མདོག་སྟོན་ཁའི་ཟླ་བ་ལྟར་དཀར་བ། ནོར་བུ་ཆུ་ཤེལ་ལྟར་དྭངས་པ། དྲི་མ་མེད་པའི་འོད་ཟེར་ཁ་དོག་ལྔ་ལྡན་དུ་འཕྲོ་བ། ཆོས་ཐམས་ཅད་དེ་བཞིན་ཉིད་དུ་རོ་གཅིག་པས་ཞལ་གཅིག་པ། ཀུན་ལ་ཁྱབ་པའི་བྱམས་བརྩེ་མངའ་བས་ཀུན་ནས་འཛུམ་པའི་མདངས་དང་ལྡན་པ། དག་པའི་སྤྱན་གྱིས་དུས་དྲུག་ཏུ་གཟིགས་པས་ཨུཏྤ་ལའི་འདབ་མ་ལྟར་རབ་ཏུ་རྒྱས་པའི་སྤྱན་མངའ་བ། ཕྱོགས་བཅུ་དུས་གསུམ་གྱི་སངས་རྒྱས་རྣམས་སེམས་ཅན་གྱི་དོན་དུ་བསྐུལ་བར་མཛད་པས་ཕྱག་དང་པོ་གཉིས་ཐུགས་ཀར་ཐལ་མོ་སྦྱར་བ། ཐུགས་རྗེའི་རྒྱུན་མི་འཆད་པའི་བརྡར་གཡས་ཀྱི་གཉིས་པ་ཤེལ་དཀར་གྱི་ཕྲེང་བ་བརྒྱ་རྩ་བརྒྱད་འདྲེན་ཚུལ་དུ་བསྣམས་པ། རང་དོན་ཡིད་བྱེད་ཀྱི་འདམ་གྱིས་མ་གོས་པས་གཡོན་གྱི་གཉིས་པས་པདྨ་དཀར་པོ་འདབ་མ་བརྒྱད་པ་ཡུ་བ་དང་བཅས་པ་སྙན་གྱི་ཐད་ཀར་ཁ་བྱེ་བ་འཛིན་པ། ཁྲེལ་ཡོད་ངོ་ཚའི་རང་བཞིན་གྱི་རས་བཟང་པོའི་ཤམ་ཐབས་ལ་ནོར་བུས་བརྒྱན་པའི་སྐ་རགས་ཀྱིས་སྒྲས་པ། སྙིང་རྗེ་དང་སྟོང་པ་ཟུང་དུ་འཇུག་པས་ཞབས་རྡོ་རྗེའི་སྐྱིལ་ཀྲུང་དུ་བཞུགས་པ། རྣམ་ཐར་བརྒྱད་ཀྱི་རང་བཞིན་རིན་པོ་ཆེའི་རྒྱན་བརྒྱན་པའི་སྐ་རགས་སྙིང་རྗེ་ཆེན་པོའི་ཉམས་དང་ལྡན་པས་རི་དྭགས་ཀྱི་པགས་པས་ནུ་མ་གཡོན་པ་བསྐབ་པ། གསོལ་བ་འདེབས་པའི་ཡུལ་བསྟན་པའི་ཕྱིར་རང་གི་བླ་མ་འོད་དཔག་མེད་ཀྱིས་རལ་པའི་ཐོར་ཚུགས་ཀྱི་ངོས་ལ་མཛེས་པར་བརྒྱན་པ། ཐུགས་རྗེ་ཆེན་པོའི་བསིལ་ཟེར་གྱིས་ཉོན་མོངས་པའི་ཚ་གདུང་ཞི་བར་མཛད་པས་དྲི་མེད་ཟླ་བ་རྒྱས་པའི་རྒྱབ་ཡོལ་ཅན། རྩ་བརྒྱུད་བླ་མ། ཡི་དམ་ལྷ་ཚོགས། སངས་རྒྱས་བྱང་སེམས་ཀུན་འདུས་ཀྱི་ངོ་བོར་བཞུགས་པ་ལ། བདག་དང་འགྲོ་དྲུག་སེམས་ཅན་ཐམས་ཅད་ཀྱིས་གུས་པ་ཆེན་པོས་གསོལ་བ་འདེབས་པར་མོས་ལ་འདི་གསུང་བར་ཞུ།

ཇོ་བོ་སྐྱོན་གྱིས་མ་གོས་སྐུ་མདོག་དཀར།།
རྫོགས་སངས་རྒྱས་ཀྱིས་དབུ་ལ་བརྒྱན།།
ཐུགས་རྗེའི་སྤྱན་གྱིས་འགྲོ་ལ་གཟིགས།།
སྤྱན་རས་གཟིགས་ལ་ཕྱག་འཚལ་ལོ།།

ཞེས་པའི་གསོལ་འདེབས་ཅི་ནུས་དང་། སྨྲོ་ན། གྲུབ་ཐོབ་ཉིད་དགེ་སློང་པདྨ་དཀར་པོར་སྐྱེ་བ་བཞེས་པའི་ཚེ་སྤྱན་རས་གཟིགས་ལ་གསོལ་བ་བཏབ་པའི་རྡོ་རྗེའི་གསུང་བྱིན་བརླབས་ཅན་དང་། བརྒྱུད་པའི་གསོལ་འདེབས་རྣམས་ཀྱང་བྱ། །གཉིས་པ་ནི། །དེ་ལྟར་གསོལ་བ་བཏབ་པས། སྤྱི་བོའི་འཕགས་པའི་སྐུ་

ལས་འོད་ཟེར་དཔག་ཏུ་མེད་པ་འཕྲོས། སྣོད་བཅུད་ཐམས་ཅད་ལ་ཕོག་པས། མ་དག་ལས་སྣང་གི་འཆར་སྒོ་སྦྱངས་ཏེ། སྣོད་ཀྱི་འཇིག་རྟེན་གཞལ་ཡས་ཁང་། བཅུད་ཀྱི་སེམས་ཅན་ཐམས་ཅད་ལུས་སྣང་སྟོང་དབྱེར་མེད་འཕགས་པའི་སྐུའི་རང་བཞིན། ངག་གྲགས་སྟོང་དབྱེར་མེད་ཡི་གེ་དྲུག་མའི་རང་སྒྲ། ཡིད་རིག་སྟོང་དབྱེར་མེད་ཡེ་ཤེས་ཀྱི་རོལ་པ་སྟེ་སྣང་གྲགས་རྟོག་གསུམ་དཀྱིལ་འཁོར་གསུམ་དུ་གནས་བསྒྱུར་བའི་མཁའ་ཁྱབ་ཀྱི་ཏིང་ངེ་འཛིན་རྒྱ་འབྱམས་ཀྱི་ངང་དུ་ཡིད་རྩེ་གཅིག་པས་ཡི་གེ་དྲུག་པའི་བཟླས་པ་ལྷན་ཅིག་ཏུ་གནང་བར་ཞུ།

ཨོཾ་མ་ཎི་པདྨེ་ཧཱུྃ།

བཟླས་ལུང་སྐབས་འདིར་ཡིག་དྲུག་བརྒྱ་རྩ་སོགས་གང་འོས་གསུང་སྒྲོལ་ཡོད་གསུངས།

ཞེས་ཡི་གེ་དྲུག་པའི་བཟླས་བརྗོད་ཇི་ཙམ་ནུས་པ་བྱ།

གསུམ་པ་ནི། སྒོམ་བཟླས་གྲུབ་པའི་མཐར། རང་སེམས་གསལ་སྟོང་རིག་པའི་སྙིང་པོ་ཅན། ཆོས་ཉིད་དོན་གྱི་ཐུགས་རྗེ་ཆེན་པོ་སྐུ་གསུམ་གདོད་ནས་རང་ཆས་སུ་གྲུབ་པ། གཞི་ལམ་འབྲས་བུའི་གནས་སྐབས་ཀུན་ཁྱབ་བདེ་གཤེགས་སྙིང་པོའི་རང་ཞལ་ལ། གཉུག་མའི་རིག་པས་བལྟ་བྱ་ལྟ་བྱེད་མ་གྲུབ་པའི་ངང་དུ་གཅེར་གྱིས་བལྟ། བཟོ་བཅོས་དགག་སྒྲུབ་ཀྱི་ཡིད་དཔྱོད་དང་བྲལ། བདེ་གསལ་མི་རྟོག་པ་སོགས་ཉམས་ཀྱི་འཛིན་སྟངས་ལ་མ་ཞེན། རྣམ་རྟོག་གཟུགས་འཛིན་གྱི་འཕྲུ་ལམ་ཐད་ཀྱིས་བཅད་དེ། རྟོག་པའི་འགྲོ་འདུ་བྱུང་ཡང་ཆོས་ཉིད་གཉུག་མའི་ངང་དུ་རང་ཞི་རང་གྲོལ་དུ་བཏང་ནས་སྤྲོས་བྲལ་གྱི་གནས་ལུགས་ལ་ཅི་གནས་སུ་མཉམ་པར་བཞག་གོ །

གསུམ་པ་རྗེས་ཀྱི་བྱ་བ་ནི། མཉམ་བཞག་དེ་ལས་ལྡང་བར་འདོད་ན། སླར་རང་ཉིད་འཕགས་པ་སྤྱན་རས་གཟིགས་ཀྱི་སྐུ་སྣང་ལ་རང་བཞིན་མེད་པར་གྱུར་པར་མོས་ལ། དགྲ་གཉེན་བར་མས་བསྡུས་པའི་འགྲོ་བ་ཐམས་ཅད་ལ་ཆགས་སྡང་རྨོངས་གསུམ་གྱིས་འདོར་ལེན་མི་བྱ་བར་གཟུགས་སུ་སྣང་བ་ཐམས་ཅད་འཕགས་པའི་སྐུའི་རང་བཞིན། སྒྲ་སྐད་གྲགས་ཚད་ཡི་གེ་དྲུག་པའི་རང་སྒྲ། བཟང་ངན་གྱི་དྲན་རྟོག་ཅི་ཤར་ཡེ་ཤེས་ཆེན་པོར་ཐག་བཅད་དེ་རྟོག་པའི་རོ་མི་སྨྱོང་བ་གང་ཤར་དེ་ཀའི་ངོ་བོ་ལ་ཧྲང་དེ་འཛོག་པ་སྟེ་ཁྱེར་སོ་གསུམ་གྱི་རྣལ་འབྱོར་དང་མ་བྲལ་བའི་ངོས། འཁྲུལ་སྣང་ལ་བདེན་པར་བཟུང་བའི་ཕ་མ་སེམས་ཅན་རིས་སུ་མ་ཆད་པ་ལ་བྱམས་དང་སྙིང་རྗེས་ཀུན་ནས་བསླངས་ཏེ། བདེན་ཞེན་བྲལ་བ་སྒྱུ་མའི་ཚུལ་གྱིས་ལུས་ངག་ཡིད་གསུམ་གྱི་སྒོ་ནས་དགེ་བའི་བྱ་བ་ཅི་ནུས་སུ་འབད། དེ་ལྟ་བུའི་དགེ་བའི་རྩ་བ་ཐམས་ཅད་ཀྱང་རབ་འཁོར་གསུམ་ཡོངས་སུ་དག་པའི་ཚུལ། འབྲིང་བདེན་མེད་སྒྱུ་མའི་བློ། ཐ་མ་རྒྱལ་བ་སྲས་བཅས་ཀྱི་རྗེས་སུ་སློབ་པའི་བསམ་པས་སེམས་ཅན་གྱི་དོན་དུ་བསྔོ་བ་འདི་ལྷན་ཅིག་ཏུ་གནང་བར་ཞུ།

དེ་ལྟར་དུ་བགྱིས་པའི་དགེ་བའི་རྩ་བ་འདི་ལ་བརྟེན་ནས་བདག་དང་ཕ་མ
སེམས་ཅན་ཐམས་ཅད་སངས་རྒྱས་ཐོབ་པར་གྱུར་ཅིག །

ཅེས་པ་དང་།

དགེ་བ་འདི་ཡིས་མྱུར་དུ་བདག །
སྤྱན་རས་གཟིགས་དབང་འགྲུབ་གྱུར་ནས།།

སོགས་བསྔོ་སྨོན་རྣམ་པར་དག་པས་རྒྱས་འདེབས་པར་བྱའོ། །དེས་བསྒོམ་ལུང་གི་རིམ་པ་ཟབ་མོ་ལེགས་པར་གསན་བ་ཡིན་པས། ཇི་ལྟར་ཕོག་པའི་དམིགས་བཟླས། དེ་ལྟ་བུ་རབ་ཐུབ་བཞིའི་རིམ་པས་ཁོར་ཡུག །འཕྲིན་སྒོམ་བཟླས་ཐུན་རེ་ཆགས་མེད། ཐམས་ཅད་ཞག་བདུན་གྱི་མཐའ་བརྟེན་པའི་ཉམས་ལེན་བྱས་པའི་ཕན་ཡོན་ནི། སྡིག་སྒྲིབ་ཉོན་མོངས་དག སྙིང་རྗེ་དང་རྟོགས་པ་འཆར། གཞན་དོན་རྒྱ་ཆེན་པོ་འགྲུབ། ཕྱི་མ་བདེ་བ་ཅན་དུ་སྐྱེས་ནས་མྱུར་དུ་འཚང་རྒྱ་བ་སོགས་སྨོས་ཀྱིས་མི་ལོངས་པ་མདོ་རྒྱུད་བསྟན་བཅོས་མཐའ་དག་ནས་གསུངས་པས་ཚོགས་ཆུང་ལ་དོན་ཆེ་བའི་གདམས་པ་འདི་ཉིད་རང་དོན་དུ་རྩེ་གཅིག་ཉམས་སུ་ལེན་པ་དང་། གཞན་ལ་འཆད་ཅིང་སྤེལ་བ་དང་། ཐ་ན་སྒྲོག་ཆགས་གྲོག་སྦུར་ཚུན་ཆད་ཀྱི་རྣ་བར་ཐུགས་རྗེ་ཆེན་པོའི་མཚན་དང་ཡིག་དྲུག་སྒྲོགས་ལ་འཁོར་བ་དོང་སྤྲུགས་འབྲེལ་ཚད་དོན་ལྡན་དོན་གཉིས་ལྷུན་གྱིས་གྲུབ་པའི་ལམ་བཟང་མཐར་དབྱུང་བར་ཞུ། བསོད་ནམས་འདི་ཡིས་ཐམས་ཅད་གཟིགས་པ་སོགས་ཀྱིས་བསྔོ་སྨོན་པས་ལ་འདུས་པ་གྱིས་སོ།

སྒོམ་བཟླས་ཡིད་ལ་དྲན་ཙམ་གྱིས།
མཚམས་མེད་སྒྲིབ་པ་ཟད་བྱེད་ཅིང་།
ཁྱད་པར་གངས་ཅན་མགོན་གཅིག་པུ།
དེ་སྒྲུབ་གདམས་ངག་གསལ་བཤད་པས།
མཐོང་ཐོས་དྲན་རེག་སྐྱེ་དགུ་ཀུན།
འོད་སྣང་མཐའ་ཡས་ཞིང་ཁམས་སུ།
འཇིག་རྟེན་མགོན་པོས་དབུགས་དབྱུང་སྟེ།
གང་གི་རྣམ་ཐར་ཀུན་འགྲུབ་ཤོག

ཅེས་པའང་དམིགས་པ་མེད་པའི་ཐུགས་རྗེ་དང་ལྡན་པ་རྗེ་བཙུན་མཉྫུ་གྷོ་ཥའི་གསུང་ཟེར་བདུད་རྩིས་སྙིང་གི་པདྨོར་དྲན་པས། ཡིག་དྲུག་པ་བློ་གྲོས་མཐའ་ཡས་ཀྱིས་རྩ་བའི་ཡིག་སྙིང་གི་དགོངས་པ་གསལ་བར་བྲིས། ལུགས་ཟབ་པའི་ཁྲིད་ཡིག་མ་བུའི་བཅུད་བསྡུས་ཏེ། ལྷག་པའི་བསམ་པས་དཔལ་སྤུངས་ཡང་ཁྲོད་དུ་སྦྱར་བས་གཞན་ཕན་ནམ་མཁའ་དང་མཉམ་པར་གྱུར་ཅིག །དགེ་ལེགས་འཕེལ།།

༄༅། །འཕགས་མཆོག་སྤྱན་རས་གཟིགས་ཀྱི་བསྒོམ་བཟླས་འགྲོ་དོན་མཁའ་ཁྱབ་མའི་ཟིན་བྲིས་ཉུང་བསྡུས་
འགྲོ་དོན་ཆར་རྒྱུན་ཞེས་བྱ་བ་བཞུགས་སོ། །

THE TIBETAN TEXT:

The Continuous Rain of Benefit to Beings

by **Khakhyab Dorje**

༄༅། །འཕགས་མཆོག་སྤྱན་རས་གཟིགས་ཀྱི་བསྒོམ་བཟླས་འགྲོ་དོན་མཁའ་ཁྱབ་མའི་ཟིན་བྲིས་ཉུང་བསྡུས་འགྲོ་དོན་ཆར་རྒྱུན་ཞེས་བྱ་བ་བཞུགས་སོ། །

སྭསྟི།
རྒྱལ་བ་ཀུན་གྱི་སྙིང་རྗེ་ཆེ།།
ཕྱག་རྒྱར་ཤར་བའི་སྤྱན་རས་གཟིགས།།
འཁོར་བ་དོང་སྤྲུག་ཕྲིན་ལས་ཅན།།
དབྱེར་མེད་རྗེ་བཙུན་མགོན་ལ་འདུད།།

འདིར་རྒྱལ་བ་ཀུན་ལས་ཐུགས་བསྐྱེད་དང་ཕྲིན་ལས་ཁྱད་པར་དུ་འཕགས་པ། ཇི་སྲིད་འཁོར་བ་མ་སྟོངས་ཀྱི་བར་དུ་ཞི་བའི་ཉིང་འཛིན་ལ་མི་གཞོལ་བར་དུས་གསུམ་རྒྱུན་གྱི་རྟག་པར་འགྲོ་དྲུག་འདྲེན་པའི་ཕྲིན་ལས་ཅན། ཁྱད་པར་རྒྱལ་བ་ཉི་མའི་གཉེན་གྱི་ལུང་བསྟན་རྗེས་སུ་གནང་བས་མདའ་གསོལ་བ་བཞིན་གདོང་དམར་ཅན་གྱི་ཡུལ། ཆེས་གདུལ་དཀའ་བའི་ལྗོངས། འཕགས་པའི་གདུལ་ཞིང་དུ་བདག་གིར་མཛད་ནས། རྒྱལ་བློན། ལོ་པཎ། གྲུབ་ཐོབ། ཁྱིའུ་ཕོ་མོ་སོགས་སྣ་ཚོགས་པའི་གཟུགས་ཀྱིས་དངོས་སུ་ཕྲིན་ལས་མཛད་ཅིང་བྱིན་གྱིས་བརླབས་པའི་མཐུ་ལས། བྱིས་པ་སླ་ཤེས་རྩུན་གྱིས་གསང་སྔགས་ཀྱི་རྒྱལ་པོ་ཡི་གེ་དྲུག་པ་མ་བསླབས་རང་རྗོལ་དུ་ཤེས་པས་མཚོན། ཁ་བ་ཅན་གྱི་ལྗོངས་འདིར་ལྷ་སྐལ་ཇོ་བོ་ཐུགས་རྗེ་ཆེན་པོ་ལས་གཞན་དུ་མ་དམིགས་པས། སྔོན་བྱོན་སྤྲུལ་པའི་སྐྱེས་མཆོག་རྣམས་ཀྱིས་འཕགས་པའི་སྒྲུབ་སྐོར་རྒྱས་བསྡུས་མཐའ་ཡས་པ་གསལ་བར་མཛད་པ་རྣམས་ལས། འདིར་སྤྱན་རས་གཟིགས་དངོས་མིའི་དོན་དུ་བྱོན་པ། གྲུབ་པའི་དབང་ཕྱུག་ཐང་སྟོང་རྒྱལ་པོས་སྤེལ་བ་འགྲོ་དོན་མཁའ་ཁྱབ་མའི་བསྒོམ་བཟླས་ཉམས་སུ་ལེན་ཚུལ་ལ། སྦྱོར་བ་སྐྱབས་འགྲོ་སེམས་བསྐྱེད། དངོས་གཞི་ལྷ་བསྒོམ་པ། སྔགས་བཟླ་བ། རྗེས་ལམ་དུ་ཁྱེར་ཞིང་དགེ་རྩ་བསྔོ་བ། ཕན་ཡོན་བསྟན་པ་སྟེ་དོན་དྲུག་གི་སྒོ་ནས་ཉམས་སུ་ལེན་པ་ལ།

དང་པོ་སྐྱབས་འགྲོ་སེམས་བསྐྱེད་ནི། མདུན་གྱི་ནམ་མཁར་འཇའ་ཐིག་མེ་ཏོག་སྤྲིན་གྱི་གློང་ན། རྩ་བའི་བླ་མ་དང་དབྱེར་མེད་པའི་འཕགས་པ་སྤྱན་

རས་གཟིགས་ཕྱོགས་དུས་ཀྱི་དཀོན་མཆོག་རྩ་གསུམ་རྒྱལ་བ་ཀུན་འདུས་ཀྱི་ངོ་བོར་མངོན་སུམ་བཞིན་བཞུགས་པའི་དྲུང་དུ། བདག་ཉིད་ཀྱི་གཙོར་བྱས། དགྲ་གཉེན་བར་མས་བསྡུས་པའི་འགྲོ་དྲུག་གི་སེམས་ཅན་ཐམས་ཅད་ཁྲིམ་ཚོགས་སུ་འཁོད་དེ་སྒོ་གསུམ་འཛུག་པ་གཅིག་པས། བདག་ཅག་རྣམས་འཁོར་བ་སྡུག་བསྔལ་གྱི་རྒྱ་མཚོ་ཆེན་པོ་ལས་སྐྱོབས་པའི་ནུས་མཐུ་བླ་མ་སྤྱན་རས་གཟིགས་ལ་མངའ་བས་རེ་ལྟོས་ཡིད་བསྐྱུར་གྱིས་དད་པ་དང་། སྐྱབ་ཏུ་གསོལ་སྙམ་པའི་འདུན་པ། སྐྱོབས་ངེས་པའི་ཡིད་ཆེས་ཏེ་གསུམ་དང་ལྡན་པའི་སྒོ་ནས།

སངས་རྒྱས་ཆོས་དང་ཚོགས་ཀྱི་མཆོག་རྣམས་ལ།།
བྱང་ཆུབ་བར་དུ་བདག་ནི་སྐྱབས་སུ་མཆི།།

ཞེས་ངག་ཏུ་གྲངས་ཅི་ལྟར་འོས་པ་བརྗོད་པས་སྐྱབས་སུ་འགྲོ་ཞིང་། དེང་ཕྱིན་བདག་དང་སེམས་ཅན་རྣམས་འཕགས་པ་ཐུགས་རྗེ་ཆེན་པོའི་སྐྱབས་འོག་ཏུ་ཚུད་ཡོད་སྙམ་པའི་ངེས་ཤེས་བརྟན་པོའང་བྱ། མདུན་དུ་དམིགས་པའི་སེམས་ཅན་དེ་རྣམས་དམིགས་ཡུལ་དུ་བྱས་ཏེ། འདི་ཐམས་ཅད་བདག་གི་ཕ་མར་མ་གྱུར་པ་ནི་གཅིག་ཀྱང་མེད་པའི་དྲིན་ཅན། བདེ་བ་སྒྲུབ་འདོད་དང་། སྡུག་བསྔལ་སྤོང་འདོད་པ་ཤ་སྟག་ཡིན་ཀྱང་། སྡུག་བསྔལ་གྱི་རྒྱུ་འབའ་ཞིག་བསྒྲུབས་པས། འབྲས་བུ་འཁོར་བ་དང་ངན་སོང་གི་སྡུག་བསྔལ་དོས་དྲག་པོས་ཐར་དུས་མེད་པར་མནར་བ་འདི་རྣམས། བདག་གིས་བདེ་བ་ཐམས་ཅད་ཀྱི་མཆོག་བླ་ན་མེད་པ་རྫོགས་པའི་སངས་རྒྱས་ཀྱི་གོ་འཕང་ལ་ཅི་ནས་ཀྱང་འགོད་པར་བྱ། དེ་ལྟ་བུ་སྒྲུབ་པའི་ནུས་པ་ད་ལྟ་བདག་ལ་མེད་པས། བདག་གིས་འཕགས་པ་སྤྱན་རས་གཟིགས་ཀྱི་བསྒོམ་བཟླས་ཟབ་མོ་ཉམས་སུ་བླངས་ནས་འཕགས་པ་མཆོག་གི་གོ་འཕང་དམ་པ་བསྒྲུབ་ཏེ། འཁོར་བ་ཇི་སྲིད་པར་འགྲོ་བའི་དོན་ལ་སྤྱན་རས་གཟིགས་ཀྱི་རྣམ་ཐར་དང་མཚུངས་པར་འཇུག་པར་བགྱིའོ་སྙམ་པའི་བཅོས་མིན་གྱི་འདུན་པ་དྲག་པོས། བླ་མ་སྤྱན་རས་གཟིགས་ཀྱི་སྤྱན་སྔར་བྱང་ཆུབ་ཏུ་སེམས་བསྐྱེད་པའི་དམ་བཅའ་བླངས་ནས།

བདག་གིས་བསྒོམ་བཟླས་བགྱིས་པའི་བསོད་ནམས་ཀྱིས།།
འགྲོ་ལ་ཕན་ཕྱིར་སངས་རྒྱས་འགྲུབ་པར་ཤོག །

ཅེས་ལན་ཁ་ཡར་བརྗོད་ཅིང་སྒོམ་དོན་བློ་ལ་གསལ་ངེས་བྱ། བླ་མ་སྤྱན་རས་གཟིགས་ཀྱི་སྐུ་ལས་འོད་ཟེར་དུ་མ་འཕྲོས། དམིགས་ཡུལ་རྣམས་ལ་ཕོག་པས་དེ་རྣམས་ཀྱི་སྡིག་སྒྲིབ་དང་སྡུག་བསྔལ་སྦྱང་ནས་བདེ་བ་དང་ལྡན་པར་བྱས། །སྐྱབས་ཡུལ་འོད་དུ་ཞུ་བ་རང་ལ་ཐིམ་པས་རྒྱུད་བྱིན་གྱིས་བརླབས་པར་བསམ་མོ།

གཉིས་པ་ལྷ་བསྒོམ་པ་ནི། བདག་ཐ་མལ་པར་གནས་པའི་མཐའ་བསྐོར་དུ་སྙིང་རྗེའི་ཡུལ་དུ་གྱུར་པའི་འགྲོ་དྲུག་སྐྱབས་འགྲོའི་སྐབས་ལྟར་གསལ་བའི།

སོ་སོའི་སྤྱི་བོར་རབ་ཏུ་རྒྱས་པའི་པདྨ་དཀར་པོ་འདབ་བརྒྱད་ཟེའུ་འབྲུ་དང་བཅས་པའི་ལྟེ་བར་ཟླ་བའི་དཀྱིལ་འཁོར་ཉ་གང་བ་དྲི་མ་མེད་པའི་སྟེང་དུ་ཧྲཱིཿཡིག་མུ་ཏིག་གི་མདོག་ལྟར་དཀར་ཞིང་འོད་འཚེར་བ། རྒྱལ་བ་ཀུན་གྱི་མཐུ་སྟོབས་གཅིག་ཏུ་བསྡུས་པའི་རང་གཟུགས་སུ་ཤར་བར་བསྒོམ། དེ་ལས་འོད་ཟླ་བའི་ཟེར་ལྟ་བུ་གྲངས་མེད་འཕྲོས། ཕྱོགས་བཅུའི་རྒྱལ་བའི་དཀྱིལ་འཁོར་མ་ལུས་པ་ལ་སྐུ་གསུང་ཐུགས་མཉེས་པའི་མཆོད་པ་འབུལ། བདག་གཞན་ཐམས་ཅད་ལ་ཕོག་པས་ནད་གདོན་སྡིག་སྒྲིབ་ཐམས་ཅད་སྦྱངས། རིགས་དྲུག་གི་གནས་ཐམས་ཅད་ལ་ཁྱབ་པས་སྡུག་བསྔལ་བསལ་ནས་བདེ་བ་ལ་བཀོད། འཕགས་པའི་ཚོགས་ཀྱི་བྱིན་རླབས་འོད་ཟེར་གྱི་རྣམ་པར་ཚུར་བསྡུས།

སྤྱི་བོའི་ཧྲཱིཿཡིག་སོ་སོ་ལ་ཐིམ་པའི་རྐྱེན་གྱིས་སྐད་ཅིག་གིས་འཕགས་མཆོག་སྤྱན་རས་གཟིགས་སྐུ་མདོག་གངས་ལ་ཉི་མ་ཤར་བ་ལྟར་ཤིན་ཏུ་དཀར་ཞིང་གསལ་ལ་འཚེར་བ་སྐུ་ལས་འོད་ཟེར་ཁ་དོག་ལྔ་ལྡན་འཕྲོ་བས་རྒྱལ་བའི་ཞིང་ཁམས་ཁྱབ་པས། འཕགས་པ་རྣམས་འགྲོ་བའི་དོན་ལ་བསྐུལ་མ་མཛད། མར་རིགས་དྲུག་གི་གནས་རྣམས་སུ་ཁྱབ་པས་སོ་སོའི་སྡུག་བསྔལ་ཐམས་ཅད་བསལ་ནས་བདེ་བ་དང་ལྡན་པར་སྦྱོར་བ། བདག་དང་སེམས་ཅན་ཐམས་ཅད་ལ་དགྱེས་པའི་འཛུམ་མདངས་དང་ལྡན་ཞིང་། བུ་གཅིག་པོ་ལ་མས་བརྩེ་བ་བཞིན་དུ་བདག་གཞན་འགྲོ་བ་རྣམས་ལ་བྱམས་བརྩེའི་ཐུགས་ཀྱི་རྟག་ཏུ་ཁྱབ་པའི་སྤྱན་རས་ཟུང་གིས་དུས་གསུམ་ཀུན་ཏུ་གཟིགས་པ། ཕྱག་བཞི་དང་པོ་གཉིས་ཐུགས་ཀར་ཐལ་མོ་སྦྱར་བ། གཡས་འོག་མས་ཤེལ་དཀར་གྱི་ཕྲེང་བ་འཛིན་ཅིང་། གཡོན་འོག་མས་པདྨ་དཀར་པོ་འདབ་མ་བརྒྱད་པ་སྡོང་བུ་དང་བཅས་པ་འཛིན་པ། དར་དཀར་པོ་གསེར་གྱི་རི་མོ་ཅན་གྱི་སྟོད་གཡོག་དང་དར་དཔྱངས་མཛེས་ཤིང་། དར་དམར་པོའི་ཤམ་ཐབས་ཅན་ཛམྦུའི་ཆུ་བོའི་གསེར་ལ་ལྷ་ཡི་རིན་པོ་ཆེ་དུ་མའི་ཕྲ་ཚོམ་གྱིས་སྤྲས་པའི་དབུ་བརྒྱན། སྙན་ཆ། མགུལ་རྒྱན། དོ་ཤལ། སེ་མོ་དོ། དཔུང་རྒྱན་དང་། ཕྱག་ཞབས་ཀྱི་གདུབ་བུ། སྒྲ་རག་གཡེར་ཁའི་ཕྲེང་བ་སྒྲད་སྙན་པར་འཁྲོལ་བ་དང་བཅས་པས་སྐུའི་ཆ་ཀུན་ལེགས་པར་བརྒྱན་པ། རི་དྭགས་ཀྲིཥྞ་ས་རའི་པགས་པ་གསེར་མདོག་ཅན་གྱིས་ནུ་མ་གཡོན་པ་བཀབ་པ། དབུ་སྐྲ་ཐོར་ཙུགས་སུ་བཅིངས་པའི་ལྷག་མ་ཐུར་དུ་གྲོལ་བ། རིགས་བདག་སངས་རྒྱས་འོད་དཔག་མེད་མཆོག་གི་སྤྲུལ་སྐུའི་ཆ་ལུགས་ཅན་གཙུག་ཏོར་གྱི་རྩེ་མོར་བཞུགས་པའི་དབུ་བརྒྱན་ཅན། ཞབས་གཉིས་རྡོ་རྗེའི་སྐྱིལ་མོ་ཀྲུང་དུ་བཞུགས་པ། དྲི་མ་མེད་ཅིང་རབ་ཏུ་རྒྱས་པ་ཟླ་བའི་རྒྱབ་ཡོལ་ལ་སྐུ་བསྟེན་པ། དུས་གསུམ་དུ་འབྱོན་ཞིང་། ཕྱོགས་བཅུར་བཞུགས་པའི་སྐྱབས་གནས་དཀོན་མཆོག་ཀུན་འདུས་ཀྱི་ངོ་བོར་བཞུགས་པར་བསམས་ལ།

བདག་སོགས་མཁའ་ཁྱབ་སེམས་ཅན་གྱི།།
སྤྱི་གཙུག་པད་དཀར་ཟླ་བའི་སྟེང་།།
ཧྲཱིཿལས་འཕགས་མཆོག་སྤྱན་རས་གཟིགས།།
དཀར་གསལ་འོད་ཟེར་ལྔ་ལྡན་འཕྲོ།།

འཛམ་ལྷན་ཐུགས་རྗེའི་སྤྱན་གྱིས་གཟིགས།།
ཕྱག་བཞིའི་དང་པོ་ཐལ་སྦྱར་མཛད།།
འོག་གཉིས་ཤེལ་ཕྲེང་པད་དཀར་བསྣམས།།
དར་དང་རིན་ཆེན་རྒྱན་གྱིས་སྤྲས།།
རི་དྭགས་པགས་པའི་སྟོད་གཡོག་གསོལ།།
འོད་དཔག་མེད་པའི་དབུ་རྒྱན་ཅན།།
ཞབས་གཉིས་རྡོ་རྗེའི་སྐྱིལ་ཀྲུང་བཞུགས།།
དྲི་མེད་ཟླ་བར་རྒྱབ་བརྟེན་པ།།
སྐྱབས་གནས་ཀུན་འདུས་ངོ་བོར་གྱུར།།

ཞེས་དལ་ཁྱུས་སྐབས་ཕྱེད་པར་བཀླག་ཅིང་སྐུའི་རྣམ་པ་རེ་རེ་ནས་གསལ་འདེབས་བྱའོ།

གསུམ་པ་སྟེགས་བཟླ་བ་ལའང་གསོལ་འདེབས་ཀྱི་སྒོ་ནས་ཐུགས་བསྐུལ་བསྐུལ་བ་དང་། སྤྲོ་བསྡུ་ལ་བརྟེན་ནས་སྒོམ་གསུམ་ལྷའི་རྣལ་འབྱོར་དུ་བྱ་བ་གཉིས་ཀྱི།

དང་པོ་ནི། དེ་ལྟར་གསལ་བའི་བླ་མ་འཕགས་མཆོག་སྤྱན་རས་གཟིགས་ལ་བདག་དང་སེམས་ཅན་ཐམས་ཅད་ཀྱི་མགྲིན་གཅིག་པ་དང་། བློ་རྩེ་གཅིག་པས་ཅི་མཛད་ཁྱེད་ཤེས་བློ་གཏད་ལིང་བསྒྱུར་གྱི་རིགས་དྲུག་འཁོར་བའི་གནས་ལས་བསྒྲལ་ནས། རྣམ་པ་ཐམས་ཅད་མཁྱེན་པའི་ས་ལ་འདྲེན་པར་མཛད་དུ་གསོལ་སྙམ་པའི་སྒོ་ནས།

ཇོ་བོ་སྐྱོན་གྱིས་མ་གོས་སྐུ་མདོག་དཀར།།
རྫོགས་སངས་རྒྱས་ཀྱིས་དབུ་ལ་བརྒྱན།།
ཐུགས་རྗེའི་སྤྱན་གྱིས་འགྲོ་ལ་གཟིགས།།
སྤྱན་རས་གཟིགས་ལ་ཕྱག་འཚལ་ལོ།།

ཞེས་ལན་བརྒྱའམ། ཉེར་གཅིག བདུན་སོགས་རྒྱུད་འཕོལ་ཞིང་། སྣང་བ་འགྱུར་ངེས་ཀྱི་བར་དུ་ཅི་ནུས་བརྗོད། །སྤྲོ་ཞིང་ནུས་ན། དགེ་སློང་མ་

དཔལ་མོས་མཛད་པའི་པོ་བསྟོད། སློབ་དཔོན་ཟླ་བས་མཛད་པའི་སྙེ་ངག་གིས་བསྟོད་པ་བྱིན་རླབས་ཅན་སོགས་འབྲེལ་ཆགས་ཤིང་། བྱིན་རླབས་ལྡན་པའི་གསོལ་འདེབས་ཅི་རིགས་སྦྱར་ནའང་ལེགས་པའི་ཡན་ལག་ཏུ་འགྱུར་སྙམ་མོ།

གཉིས་པ་སྤྲོ་བསྡུ་ལ་བརྟེན་ནས་སྒོ་གསུམ་ལྷའི་རྣལ་འབྱོར་དུ་བསྒྲུབ་པ་ནི། དེ་ལྟར་རྩེ་གཅིག་པའི་ཡིད་ཀྱིས་གསོལ་བ་བཏབ་ཅིང་ཐུགས་བརྒྱུད་བསྐུལ་བ་ལ་བརྟེན་ནས། སྤྱི་བོའི་འཕགས་པའི་སྐུ་ལས་འོད་ཟེར་ཁ་དོག་ལྔ་ལྡན་དཀར་པོ་ཤས་ཆེ་བ་དཔག་ཏུ་མེད་པ་འཕྲོས། བདག་དང་སེམས་ཅན་རྣམས་ལ་ཕོག་པ་ཙམ་གྱིས་སྒྲོན་མེའི་འོད་ཀྱི་མུན་པ་བསལ་བ་ལྟར། རང་གཞན་གྱི་རྒྱུད་ལ་ཐོག་མེད་ནས་བསགས་པའི་མཚམས་མེད་ལྔ་དང་། ལུས་ཀྱི་སྒོ་ནས་སྲོག་བཅད་པ། མ་བྱིན་པ་བླངས་པ། མི་ཚངས་པ་སྤྱོད་པ། ངག་གི་སྒོ་ནས་བླ་མ་དང་ཕ་རོལ་པོ་ལ་གནོད་པར་འགྱུར་བའི་རྫུན་རྫམ་པོ་ཆེ་སོགས་སྨྲས་པ་དང་། ཕན་ཚུན་འབྱེད་པའི་ཕྲ་མ། གཞན་གྱི་ཞེ་ལ་གནོད་པའི་ཚིག་རྩུབ། དོན་མེད་ཀྱི་ངག་འཁྱལ་དང་བཞི། ཡིད་ཀྱི་སྒོ་ནས་གཞན་གྱི་དཔལ་འབྱོར་རང་ལ་བྱུང་ན་སྙམ་པའི་བརྣབ་སེམས། ཕ་རོལ་པོ་ལ་གནོད་པར་འགྱུར་བའི་ཐབས་ལ་བསམ་པ་གནོད་སེམས། ཐར་པའི་ཕན་ཡོན་དང་སྡིག་པའི་ཉེས་དམིགས་མི་བདེན་ཅིང་མེད་པར་ལྟ་བ་ལོག་ལྟ་སྟེ་གསུམ་བཅས། མི་དགེ་བ་བཅུ་ཆ་མཐུན་དང་བཅས་པ་ནི་སྡིག་པ་དང་། འདོད་ཆགས། ཞེ་སྡང་། གཏི་མུག ང་རྒྱལ། ཕྲག་དོག་སྒོ་ནས་སྤྱངས་བྱ་ཁྲིམས་སུ་བཅས་པ་དང་། མ་བཅས་ཀྱང་ཉེས་པའི་གྲལ་དུ་ཡོད་པ། རང་བཞིན་གྱི་ཁ་ན་མ་ཐོ་བ་མཐོ་རིས་ཀྱི་བདེ་བ་དང་། ཐར་པའི་ལམ་ལ་སྒྲིབ་པར་གྱུར་པའི་སྒྲིབ་པ་དང་། སོ་ཐར། བྱང་སེམས། གསང་སྔགས་ཀྱི་སྡོམ་པ་བླངས་ནས་མ་གྲུས་པ་དང་། བག་མེད་པའི་དབང་དུ་བཏང་ནས་མ་སྲུང་བའི་གནས་སྐབས་ངན་འགྲོར་ལྟུང་བར་འགྱུར་བས་ན་ལྟུང་བ་དང་། བསླབ་པ་ཕྲ་མོའི་གནས་དང་འགལ་བས་ངན་འགྲོར་མི་ལྟུང་ཡང་བྱང་ཆུབ་ཐོབ་པའི་དུས་འགྱུར་བར་བྱེད་པ་སོགས་ཉེས་པའི་ཚོགས་ཏེ། མ་དག་ཅིང་ལས་ངན་པའི་སྡིག་སྒྲིབ་དང་ཉོན་མོངས་པས་བསྐྱེད་པའི་ཉེས་ལྟུང་ཅི་མཆིས་པ་སྐད་ཅིག་དེ་ཉིད་ལ་དག་ཐོག་མེད་ནས་བདག་གཞན་གཉིས་སྣང་གི་གཟུང་འཛིན་འཁྲུལ་པའི་བག་ཆགས་ཤེས་བྱའི་སྒྲིབ་པ་དང་བཅས་པ་སྦྱངས་ནས། འཕགས་པ་སྤྱན་རས་གཟིགས་ཀྱི་སྐུ་གསུང་ཐུགས་དང་དབྱེར་མེད་རོལ་པར་བྱིན་གྱིས་བརླབས་ནས་འཕགས་པའི་སྐུ་སྣང་སྟོང་འཇའ་ཚོན་ལྟ་བུར་ལམ་སྐྱེ་གྱུར། ནམ་མཁའ་དང་མཉམ་པའི་འགྲོ་བ་རིགས་དྲུག་གི་གནས་ཐམས་ཅད་ལ་ཁྱབ་པས། སྣང་བའི་ཡུལ་ཕྱི་སྣོད་ཀྱི་འཇིག་རྟེན་ཐམས་ཅད་འོག་མིན་བདེ་བ་ཅན་གྱི་ཞིང་ཁམས་ས་རྫོ་རི་བྲག་གི་མིང་མེད་པ། རིན་པོ་ཆེ་དང་། འཇའ་འོད་ཟེར་ཐིག་གི་རང་བཞིན། ནང་བཅུད་འགྲོ་དྲུག་གི་སེམས་ཅན་ཐམས་ཅད་རང་རང་གི་སྡུག་བསྔལ་ལས་གྲོལ་ཏེ། ལུས་འཕགས་པ་ཐུགས་རྗེ་ཆེན་པོའི་སྐུར་ལམ་གྱིས་གྱུར། སྐྱེ་འགྲོའི་ངག་དང་འབྱུང་བའི་སྒྲ་གྲགས་པ་ཐམས་ཅད་གསང་སྔགས་ཡི་གེ་དྲུག་མའི་རང་སྒྲ་ཨུ་རུ་རུ། དྲན་རྟོག་སེམས་ཀྱི་འཁྲུལ་ཆ་དག་ནས་འཕགས་པའི་ཐུགས་རིག་སྟོང་དབྱེར་མེད་ཀྱི་དགོངས་པ་མངོན་དུ་གྱུར་པར་བསམ། དེ་ལྟར་སྐུ་དང་ཞིང་ཁམས་སུ་ཤར་

པ་དག་པའི་སྣང་ཆ། གསང་སྔགས་ཀྱི་སྒྲ། ཐུགས་རིག་སྟོང་རྗེན་པ་རྣམས་ཀྱང་བདག་གཞན་ལུས་ངག་ཡིད་ཀྱི་སྣང་བ་རྣམས་གཉིས་སུ་མེད་ཅིང་། འཛིན་པ་དང་བྲལ་བའི་བློ་འདས་ཁྱབ་གདལ་ཆེན་པོ་ལ་འཇོག་བཞིན་དུ།

དེ་ལྟར་རྩེ་གཅིག་གསོལ་བཏབ་པས།།
འཕགས་པའི་སྐུ་ལས་འོད་ཟེར་འཕྲོས།།
མ་དག་ལས་སྣང་འཁྲུལ་ཤེས་སྦྱངས།།
ཕྱི་སྣོད་བདེ་བ་ཅན་གྱི་ཞིང་།།
ནང་བཅུད་སྐྱེ་འགྲོའི་ལུས་ངག་སེམས།།
སྤྱན་རས་གཟིགས་དབང་སྐུ་གསུང་ཐུགས།།
སྣང་གྲགས་རིག་སྟོང་དབྱེར་མེད་གྱུར།།

ཅེས་བརྗོད་ཅིང་གོང་དུ་བཤད་པའི་དམིགས་པ་རྣམས་གསལ་བཏབ་ནས། ཨོཾ་མ་ཎི་པདྨེ་ཧཱུྃ། །ཞེས་བཟླས་བརྗོད་ཐུན་གྱི་དངོས་གཞིར་བྱ། གསང་སྔགས་ཡི་གེ་དྲུག་པ་འདི་ནི། སངས་རྒྱས་ཀུན་གྱི་ཡེ་ཤེས་ཀྱི་མཐུ་གཅིག་ཏུ་བསྡུས་པ་འཕགས་པ་སྤྱན་རས་གཟིགས། དེའི་ཐུགས་རྗེ་དང་ཕྲིན་ལས་ཐམས་ཅད་ཀྱི་ནུས་སྟོབས་གཅིག་ཏུ་བསྡུས་ཤིང་ཕྱུངས་པ་གསང་སྔགས་ཡི་གེ་དྲུག་མ་འདི་ཉིད་དེ།

ཨོཾ་དཀར་པོ་ནི། འཕགས་པའི་ཡེ་ཤེས་ལྷའི་རང་རྩལ་ལས་ཤར་བ་ཡོན་ཏན་འདུས་པའི་ཡི་གེ་བསམ་གཏན་གྱི་ཕ་རོལ་ཏུ་ཕྱིན་པའི་རང་བཞིན། རྒྱུ་ཉོན་མོངས་པ་ང་རྒྱལ་དང་། དེས་བསྐྱེད་པའི་འབྲས་བུ་སྐྱི་དང་། ཁྱད་པར་ལྷ་འཕོ་ལྟུང་གི་སྡུག་བསྔལ་སྦྱོང་བར་བྱེད་པ། ལྷའི་ཐུབ་པ་དབང་པོ་བརྒྱ་བྱིན་གྱི་སྐུ་དང་ཕྲིན་ལས་གཉིས་སུ་མེད་པ། མཉམ་པ་ཉིད་ཀྱི་ཡེ་ཤེས་ཀྱི་རང་མདངས་གཟུགས་སུ་ཤར་བ། འགྲོ་དྲུག་ལྷོ་དཔལ་དང་ལྡན་པའི་ཞིང་དུ་འདྲེན་ཅིང་། སངས་རྒྱས་རིན་ཆེན་འབྱུང་ལྡན་གྱི་སྐུ་ཐོབ་པར་བྱེད་པའོ།

མ་ལྗང་ཁུ་ནི། འཕགས་པའི་ཐུགས་རྗེས་འགྲོ་བ་ཀུན་ལ་བྱམས་པ་ཚད་མེད་པའི་རྩལ་ལས་ཤར་བ་ཕྲིན་ལས་ཀྱི་ཡི་གེ་བཟོད་པའི་ཕ་རོལ་ཏུ་ཕྱིན་པའི་རང་བཞིན། རྒྱུ་ཉོན་མོངས་པ་ཕྲག་དོག་དང་། དེས་བསྐྱེད་པའི་འབྲས་བུ་སྐྱི་དང་། ཁྱད་པར་ལྷ་མིན་འཐབ་རྩོད་ཀྱི་སྡུག་བསྔལ་སྦྱོང་བར་བྱེད་པ། ལྷ་མིན་གྱི་ཐུབ་པ་ཐག་བཟང་རིས་ཀྱི་སྐུ་དང་ཕྲིན་ལས་གཉིས་སུ་མེད་པ། བྱ་བ་གྲུབ་པའི་ཡེ་ཤེས་ཀྱི་རང་མདངས་གཟུགས་སུ་ཤར་བ། འགྲོ་དྲུག་བྱང་ལས་རབ་རྫོགས་པའི་ཞིང་དུ་

འདྲེན་ཅིང༌། སངས་རྒྱས་དོན་ཡོད་གྲུབ་པའི་སྐུ་ཐོབ་པར་བྱེད་པའོ།

ཆེ་སེར་པོ་ནི། འཕགས་པའི་ཐུགས་རྗེ་རྩོལ་མེད་ཀུན་ཁྱབ་ཆེན་པོའི་རྩལ་ལས་ཤར་བ། སྐུ་གསུང་ཐུགས་ཕྲིན་ལས་ཀུན་འདུས་ཡེ་ཤེས་རྡོ་རྗེ། འཁོར་བ་མྱང་འདས་ཀྱི་དབྱིངས་སུ་རང་སར་བཟློག་པའི་ཡི་གེ ཚུལ་ཁྲིམས་ཀྱི་ཕ་རོལ་ཏུ་ཕྱིན་པའི་རང་བཞིན། རྒྱུ་གཉིས་འཛིན་མ་རིག་པའི་དྲི་མ་དང༌། དེས་བསྐྱེད་པའི་འབྲས་བུ་སྒྲི་དང༌། ཁྱད་པར་མི་སྐྱེ་རྒ་ན་འཆིའི་སྡུག་བསྔལ་གྱི་ཆུ་བོ་ཆེན་པོ་བཞི་སྦྱོང་བར་བྱེད་པ། མིའི་ཐུབ་པ་ཤཱཀྱ་ཐུབ་པའི་སྐུ་དང་ཕྲིན་ལས་གཉིས་སུ་མེད་པ། རང་བྱུང་ཡེ་ཤེས་ཀྱི་རང་མདངས་གཟུགས་སུ་ཤར་བ། འགྲོ་དྲུག་འོག་མིན་ཆོས་ཀྱི་དབྱིངས་རྣམ་པར་དག་པའི་ཞིང་དུ་འདྲེན་ཅིང༌། སངས་རྒྱས་དྲུག་པ་རྡོ་རྗེ་འཆང་གི་སྐུ་ཐོབ་པར་བྱེད་པའོ།

པད་མཐིང་ག་ནི། འཕགས་པའི་ཐུགས་རྗེ་ཕྱོགས་ལྷུང་མེད་པ་བཏང་སྙོམས་ཚད་མེད་པའི་རང་རྩལ་ལས་ཤར་བ་སྐུའི་ཡི་གེ ཤེས་རབ་ཀྱི་ཕ་རོལ་ཏུ་ཕྱིན་པའི་རང་བཞིན། རྒྱུ་ཉོན་མོངས་པ་གཏི་མུག་དང༌། དེས་བསྐྱེད་པའི་འབྲས་བུ་སྒྲི་དང༌། ཁྱད་པར་དུད་འགྲོ་གླེན་ལྐུག་བཀོལ་སྤྱོད་ཀྱི་སྡུག་བསྔལ་སྦྱོང་བར་བྱེད་པ། བྱོལ་སོང་གི་ཐུབ་པ་སེང་གེ་རབ་བརྟན་གྱི་སྐུ་དང་ཕྲིན་ལས་གཉིས་སུ་མེད་པ། ཆོས་དབྱིངས་ཡེ་ཤེས་ཀྱི་རང་མདངས་གཟུགས་སུ་ཤར་བ། འགྲོ་དྲུག་དབུས་ཕྱོགས་སྟུག་པོ་བཀོད་པའི་ཞིང་དུ་འདྲེན་ཅིང༌། སངས་རྒྱས་རྣམ་པར་སྣང་མཛད་ཀྱི་སྐུ་ཐོབ་པར་བྱེད་པའོ།

མེ་དམར་པོ་ནི། འཕགས་པའི་ཐུགས་རྗེ་ཀུན་ལ་སྙོམས་པ་དགའ་བ་ཚད་མེད་ཀྱི་རང་རྩལ་ལས་ཤར་བ་གསུང་གི་ཡི་གེ །སྦྱིན་པའི་ཕ་རོལ་ཏུ་ཕྱིན་པའི་རང་བཞིན། རྒྱུ་འདོད་ཆགས་སེར་སྣ་དང༌། དེས་བསྐྱེད་པའི་འབྲས་བུ་སྒྲི་དང༌། ཁྱད་པར་བཀྲེས་སྐོམ་ཡི་དྭགས་ཀྱི་སྡུག་བསྔལ་སྦྱོང་བར་བྱེད་པ། ཡི་དྭགས་ཀྱི་ཐུབ་པ་ཁ་ལ་མེ་འབར་གྱི་སྐུ་དང་ཕྲིན་ལས་གཉིས་སུ་མེད་པ། སོར་རྟོགས་ཡེ་ཤེས་ཀྱི་རང་མདངས་གཟུགས་སུ་ཤར་བ། འགྲོ་དྲུག་ནུབ་ཕྱོགས་བདེ་བ་ཅན་གྱི་ཞིང་དུ་འདྲེན་ཅིང༌། སངས་རྒྱས་སྣང་བ་མཐའ་ཡས་ཀྱི་སྐུ་ཐོབ་པར་བྱེད་པའོ།

ཧཱུྃ་ནག་པོ་ནི། འཕགས་པའི་ཐུགས་རྗེ་འགྲོ་བ་ཀུན་ལ་བུ་ལྟར་གཟིགས་པའི་སྙིང་རྗེ་ཚད་མེད་ཀྱི་རང་རྩལ་ལས་ཤར་བ་ཐུགས་ཀྱི་ཡི་གེ ཤེས་རབ་ཀྱི་ཕ་རོལ་ཏུ་ཕྱིན་པའི་རང་བཞིན། རྒྱུ་གཉིས་འཛིན་ཞེ་སྡང་གིས་བསྐྱེད་པའི་འབྲས་བུ་སྒྲི་དང༌། ཁྱད་པར་དམྱལ་བ་ཚ་གྲང་གི་སྡུག་བསྔལ་སྦྱོང་བར་བྱེད་པ། དམྱལ་བའི་ཐུབ་པ་ཆོས་ཀྱི་རྒྱལ་པོའི་སྐུ་དང་ཕྲིན་ལས་གཉིས་སུ་མེད་པ། མེ་ལོང་ཡེ་ཤེས་ཀྱི་རང་མདངས་གཟུགས་སུ་ཤར་བ། འགྲོ་དྲུག་མངོན་པར་དགའ་བའི་ཞིང་དུ་འདྲེན་ཅིང་སངས་རྒྱས་མི་བསྐྱོད་པའི་སྐུ་ཐོབ་པར་བྱེད་པ་སྟེ།

དེ་ལྟ་བུའི་རིགས་དྲུག་འཁོར་བ་དོང་སྤྲུགས་ཀྱི་ཕྲིན་ལས་ཚད་མེད་པའི་མཐུ་སྟོབས་ཐམས་ཅད་གཅིག་ཏུ་བསྡུས་པ། གསང་སྔགས་ཀྱི་རྒྱལ་པོ་ཡི་གེ་དྲུག་པ་འདི་ཉིད་ཐུན་གྱི་དངོས་གཞིར་ཇི་ཙམ་ནུས་པར་བཟླ།

མཐར་སྐྱེ་བོའི་བླ་མའི་སྐུའི་འོད་ཀྱིས་སྣང་སྲིད་ཐམས་ཅད་སྐུ་དང་ཞིང་ཁམས་སུ་གསལ་བ་འོད་དུ་ཞུ་ནས་བླ་མ་སྤྱན་རས་གཟིགས་ལ་ཐིམ། དེ་འོད་དུ་ཞུ་ནས་རང་ལ་ཐིམ། རང་ཡང་འོད་དུ་ཞུ་ནས་བདག་གཞན་ལྷ་སྔགས་སུ་འཛིན་པའི་འཁོར་གསུམ་མི་དམིགས་པའི་འོད་གསལ་སྟོང་པ་ཉིད། ཡོད་མེད། ཡིན་མིན། སྟོང་དང་མི་སྟོང་གི་སྤྲོས་པའི་མཚན་མའི་དམིགས་གཏད་ཐམས་ཅད་སྤངས་པ། སྣང་གྲགས་རིག་སྟོང་དབྱེར་མེད་བརྗོད་བྲལ་བ་འཕགས་པའི་ཐུགས་ཆོས་དབྱིངས་ཁྱབ་བདལ་ཆེན་པོའི་རང་ངོ་ལ་ཅི་གནས་སུ་མཉམ་པར་འཇོག་གོ

བཞི་པ་རྗེས་ལམ་དུ་ཁྱེར་བ་ནི། དེ་ལས་ལྡང་བ་ན། བདག་གཞན་དུ་སྣང་བའི་དངོས་པོ་ས་རྡོ་རི་བྲག་ལ་སོགས་པ་འབྱུང་བ་ལྔའི་ཁམས་ཀྱི་བསྡུས་པ་ཐམས་ཅད་འཕགས་པ་ཐུགས་རྗེ་ཆེན་པོའི་སྐུ་དང་། སྲོག་གི་དབང་པོས་ཟིན་པ་འགྲོ་བ་སེམས་ཅན་དང་། མ་ཟིན་པ་འབྱུང་བའི་སྒྲ་སྐད་ཐམས་ཅད་འཕགས་པའི་གསུང་ཡི་གེ་དྲུག་མའི་སྒྲ་དབྱངས། དྲན་རྟོག་ཐམས་ཅད་འཕགས་པའི་ཐུགས་རིག་སྟོང་སྤྲོས་བྲལ་ཆོས་སྐུའི་གཤིས་ལུགས་སུ་མཉམ་པར་འཇོག་པ་སྟེ། འགྲོ་འཆགས་ཉལ་འདུག་སྨྲ་བརྗོད་སྤྱོད་ལམ་ཐམས་ཅད་ལ་ཐ་མལ་གྱི་ཞེན་རྟོག་སྤངས་ནས། ཁྱེར་སོ་གསུམ་གྱི་ངང་དེ་འཛིན་འདི་ཉིད་ཀྱིས་རྗེས་ཟིན་པར་བྱས་ལ།

བདག་གཞན་ལུས་སྣང་འཕགས་པའི་སྐུ།།
སྒྲ་གྲགས་ཡི་གེ་དྲུག་མའི་དབྱངས།།
དྲན་རྟོག་ཡེ་ཤེས་ཆེན་པོའི་ཀློང་།།

ཞེས་བརྗོད།

ལྔ་པ་དགེ་རྩ་བྱང་ཆུབ་ཏུ་བསྔོ་ཞིང་སྨོན་ལམ་གདབ་པ་ནི། དེ་ལྟར་བསྒོམ་བཟླས་བགྱིས་པ་འདིས་མཚོན་བདག་རྒྱུད་ལ་ཡོད་པའི་དགེ་ཚོགས་རྣམས། སེམས་ཅན་ཐམས་ཅད་ལ་མཉམ་པ་ཉིད་དུ་བསྔོས་པའི་བསོད་ནམས་ཀྱི་ཚོགས་བླ་ན་མེད་པ་འདིས་དུས་མྱུར་བ་ཉིད་དུ་བདག་སྤྱན་རས་གཟིགས་དབང་ཕྱུག་དང་མཚུངས་པའི་གོ་འཕང་བླ་ན་མེད་པ་ཐོབ་ནས། ནམ་མཁའ་དང་མཉམ་པའི་འགྲོ་བ་གཅིག་ཀྱང་མ་ལུས་པ་འཕགས་མཆོག་ཐུགས་རྗེ་ཆེན་པོའི་གོ་འཕང་དང་དབྱེར་མེད་རྫོགས་པའི་བྱང་ཆུབ་དམ་པར་འགོད་ནུས་པའི་མཐུ་ཐོབ་པར་ཤོག་ཅིག་སྙམ་པས།

དགེ་བ་འདི་ཡིས་མྱུར་དུ་བདག །
སྤྱན་རས་གཟིགས་དབང་འགྲུབ་གྱུར་ནས།།
འགྲོ་བ་གཅིག་ཀྱང་མ་ལུས་པ།།
དེ་ཡི་ས་ལ་འགོད་པར་ཤོག །

ཅེས་དང་། གཞན་ཡང་སྨོན་ལམ་རྣམ་པར་དག་པའི་མཚམས་སྦྱོར་ཅི་ནུས་སུ་བྱའོ། །དེ་ཙམ་མི་ལྕོགས་པའི་རིགས་རྣམས་ཀྱིས། ཐོག་མར་

སྐྱབས་སེམས་སྔར་བཤད་པ་བཞིན་དང་། དངོས་གཞི་རང་གི་སྤྱི་བོར་འཕགས་མཆོག་སྤྱན་རས་གཟིགས་མངོན་རྫོགས་དང་མཐུན་པའི་སྐུ་བཞུགས་ཡོད་སྙམ་པའི་གསོལ་འདེབས་ཀྱི་དམིགས་པ་ལ་རྩེ་གཅིག་ཏུ་བློ་སྒྲིམ་ནས་གསོལ་འདེབས་ཁ་ཤས་དང་། བླ་མ་སྤྱན་རས་གཟིགས་ཁྱེད་མཁྱེན་ནོ་བསམ་པ་དང་། ཡང་ན་ཨོཾ་ནི་སྐུ་ལྔའི་ཡེ་ཤེས་འདུས་པའི་ཡི་གེ མ་ཎི་ནི་ ནོར་བུ། པདྨེ་པདྨ་ཅན་སྟེ། ནོར་བུ་པདྨ་ཅན་ཞེས་འཕགས་པ་སྤྱན་རས་ཟིགས་ཀྱི་མཚན ། ཧཱུྃ་ནི་འགྲོ་དྲུག་གི་སྡུག་བསྔལ་ལས་སྐྱོབས་པར་མཛད་པའི་ཕྲིན་ལས་ཀྱིས་སོ། དེ་ལྟར་ན། སྐུ་ལྔ་ཡེ་ཤེས་ལྔའི་བདག་ཉིད་ནོར་བུ་པདྨ་ཅན་གྱིས་འགྲོ་བ་རིགས་དྲུག་གི་སྡུག་བསྔལ་ལས་སྐྱབས་ཏུ་གསོལ་སྙམ་པའི་གསོལ་འདེབས་ཀྱི་ངང་ནས་ཡིག་དྲུག་ཅི་ནུས་བཟླ།

མཐར་སྤྱི་བོའི་བླ་མ་སྤྱན་རས་གཟིགས་དགྱེས་པ་ཆེན་པོས་འོད་དུ་ཞུ་ནས་རང་ལ་ཐིམ་པས། རང་གི་རྒྱུད་ལ་འཕགས་པའི་ཡེ་ཤེས་ཞུགས་བྱུང་སྙམ་པའི་འདུན་པ་ཐེ་ཚོམ་མེད་པར་བྱ་ཞིང་། རྗེས་བསྔོ་བ་དང་། སྨོན་ལམ་བཅས་བགྱིས་ནའང་འོག་ནས་འབྱུང་བའི་ཕན་ཡོན་རྣམས་ཐོབ་ངེས་པས་གུས་སྤྲོ་ལྡན་པས་ཀུན་གྱིས་ཉམས་ལེན་མཛོད་ཅིག།

དྲུག་པ་ཕན་ཡོན་བསྟན་པ་ནི། དེ་ལྟར་འཕགས་པ་སྤྱན་རས་གཟིགས་ཀྱི་སྒོམ་བཟླས་བགྱིས་པའི་ཕན་ཡོན་ཚད་བཟུང་མེད་པའི་སྙིང་པོ་ཙམ་ཟད་ཙམ་བརྗོད་ན། སྐུ་བསྒོམ་ཞིང་ཡིད་ལ་བྱས་པའི་ཕན་ཡོན་ནི། རྩ་རྒྱུད་པདྨ་དྲྭ་བ་ལས།

སྐུ་ཡི་དཀྱིལ་འཁོར་གཅིག་བསྒོམ་པས།།
སངས་རྒྱས་ཐམས་ཅད་འདུས་པ་ནི།།
མགོན་པོ་སྤྱན་རས་གཟིགས་སྐུ་ཡིན།།
སྒོམ་དང་ཡིད་ལ་དྲན་པས་ཀྱང་།།
མཚམས་མེད་སྡིག་པ་འདག་པར་བྱེད།།

ཅེས་དང་། གསང་སྔགས་ཀྱི་རྒྱལ་པོ་ཡི་གེ་དྲུག་པ་བཟླས་པའི་ཕན་ཡོན་ནི། རྒྱལ་བ་རྫོགས་པའི་སངས་རྒྱས་ཤཱཀྱ་ཐུབ་པའི་གསུང་དྲི་མ་མེད་པ། མ་ཎི་བཀའ་འབུམ་རིན་པོ་ཆེ་ལས་འབྱུང་གནས་ཀྱིས་བོད་འབངས་ལ་ཞལ་ཆེམས་སུ་སྩལ་བ། སྤྲུལ་པའི་གཏེར་ཆེན་རྫོང་བྲལ་རིག་འཛིན་འཇའ་ཚོན་སྙིང་པོའི་གཏེར་ཆོས་ལས།

ཨོཾ་མ་ཎི་པདྨེ་ཧཱུྃ༔ ཡི་གེ་དྲུག་པ་འདི་ནི༔ སངས་རྒྱས་ཐམས་ཅད་ཀྱི་དགོངས་པ་གཅིག་ཏུ་བསྡུས་པའི་བདག་ཉིད༔ ཆོས་ཀྱི་

ཕུང་པོ་བརྒྱད་ཁྲི་བཞི་སྟོང་གི་རྩ་བ་ཐམས་ཅད་གཅིག་ཏུ་བསྡུས་པའི་སྙིང་པོ་སངས་རྒྱས་རིགས་ལྔ་དངཿ གསང་བའི་བདག་པོ་རྣམས་ཀྱི་སྙིང་པོཿ ཡི་གེ་དྲུག་རེ་རེ་ནས་བསྡུས་པའི་མན་ངགཿ བདེ་གཤེགས་དང་ཡོན་ཏན་ཐམས་ཅད་ཀྱི་འབྱུང་གནསཿ ཕན་བདེའི་དངོས་གྲུབ་ཐམས་ཅད་ཀྱི་རྩ་བཿ མཐོ་རིས་དང་ཐར་པའི་ལམ་ཆེན་པོ་ཡིན་ནོཿ ཆོས་ཐམས་ཅད་ཀྱི་སྙིང་པོ་གསུང་མཆོག་ཡི་གེ་དྲུག་པ་འདི་ལན་གཅིག་ཐོས་པས་ཀྱངཿ ཕྱིར་མི་ལྡོག་པའི་ས་ཐོབ་སྟེཿ འགྲོ་བ་སྒྲོལ་བའི་དེད་དཔོན་དུ་འགྱུར་རོཿ གྲོག་སྦུར་རམ་དུད་འགྲོ་འཆི་ཀ་མའི་རྣ་བར་ཐོས་ནའང་ལུས་དེ་ལས་གྲོལ་ཏེ་བདེ་བ་ཅན་དུ་སྐྱེ་བར་འགྱུར་རོཿ ཡི་གེ་དྲུག་པ་དྲན་པ་ཙམ་གྱིས་ཀྱངཿ གངས་ལ་ཉི་མ་ཤར་བ་དང་འདྲ་སྟེཿ ཐོག་མ་མེད་པ་ནས་བསགས་པའི་ལས་ངན་གྱི་སྡིག་སྒྲིབ་ཐམས་ཅད་དག་ནས་བདེ་བ་ཅན་དུ་སྐྱེ་བར་འགྱུར་རོཿ རེག་ན་ཡང་སངས་རྒྱས་དང་བྱང་ཆུབ་སེམས་དཔའ་དཔག་ཏུ་མེད་པའི་དབང་བསྐུར་ཐོབ་པ་ཡིན་ནོཿ ལན་གཅིག་བསྒོམ་པས་ཀྱང་ཐོས་བསམ་སྒོམ་གསུམ་གོ་ཆོད་པ་ཡིན་ཏེཿ སྣང་ཚད་ཆོས་སྐུར་ཤརཿ འགྲོ་དོན་ཕྲིན་ལས་ཀྱི་གཏེར་ཁ་བྱེ་བ་ཡིན་ནོཿ

ཞེས་སོགས་དང་།

རིགས་ཀྱི་བུ་རིའི་རྒྱལ་པོ་རི་རབ་འདི་སྲང་ལ་གཞལ་བའི་ཚད་བགྲང་བར་ནུས་ཀྱིཿ ཡི་གེ་དྲུག་པ་ལན་གཅིག་བཟླས་པའི་བསོད་ནམས་ནི་བགྲང་བར་མི་ནུས་སོཿ རྡོ་རྗེའི་བྲག་ལ་ཀ་ཤི་ཀའི་རས་ཀྱིས་ལོ་བརྒྱ་ན་ལན་རེ་རེ་ཕྱིས་པ་ནའང་ཟད་པར་ནུས་ཏེཿ ཡི་གེ་དྲུག་པ་འདི་ལན་གཅིག་བཟླས་པའི་བསོད་ནམས་ནི་བགྲང་བར་མི་ནུས་སོཿ རྒྱ་མཚོ་ཆེན་པོའི་ཆུ་ཐིག་པ་རེ་རེ་ནས་འབྱིན་པར་ནུས་ཏེཿ ཡི་གེ་དྲུག་པ་ལན་གཅིག་བཟླས་པའི་བསོད་ནམས་ནི་ཟད་པར་མི་ནུས་སོཿ ཁ་བ་ཅན་གྱི་རྡུལ་གྱི་ཕྲ་རབ་དངཿ རྩི་ཤིང་ནགས་ཚལ་གྱི་ལོ་མ་རེ་རེ་ནས་བགྲང་བར་ནུས་ཏེཿ ཡི་གེ་དྲུག་པ་ལན་གཅིག་བཟླས་པའི་བསོད་ནམས་ཀྱི་ཚད་ནི་བགྲང་བར་མི་ནུས་སོཿ དེ་བཞིན་དུ་ཁང་པ་དཔག་ཚད་བརྒྱ་པ་ཏིལ་གྱིས་བཀང་སྟེ་ཉིན་རེ་ཏོག་པོ་རེ་རེ་བསྐྱུར་ནའང་ཟད་པར་ནུས་སྟེཿ ཡི་གེ་དྲུག་པ་ལན་གཅིག་བཟླས་པའི་བསོད་ནམས་ཀྱི་ཚད་ནི་བགྲང་བར་མི་ནུས་སོཿ ཟླ་བ་བཅུ་གཉིས་སུ་ཆར་འབབ་པའི་ཐིག་པ་རེ་རེ་ནས་བགྲང་བར་ནུས་ཀྱིཿ ཡི་གེ་དྲུག་པ་ལན་གཅིག་བཟླས་པའི་བསོད་ནམས་ཀྱི་ཚད་ནི་བགྲང་བར་མི་ནུས་སོཿ འདི་ལྟ་སྟེཿ རིགས་ཀྱི་བུ་ཉིན་མཚན་མེད་པར་མང་དུ་བརྗོད་མི་དགོས་ཀྱངཿ ང་དང་འདྲ་བའི་དེ་བཞིན་གཤེགས

པ་བྱེ་བ་ལ་བསྙེན་བཀུར་བྱས་པའི་བསོད་ནམས་ཀྱི་ཚད་ནི་བགྲང་བར་ནུས་ཏེ༔ ཡི་གེ་དྲུག་མ་ལན་གཅིག་བཟླས་པའི་བསོད་ནམས་ཀྱི་ཚད་ནི་བགྲང་བར་མི་ནུས་སོ༔ འགྲོ་བ་དྲུག་གི་སྐྱེ་སྒོ་ཡང་འདིས་གཅོད་པ་ཡིན་ནོ༔ ཕ་རོལ་ཏུ་ཕྱིན་པ་དྲུག་གི་ལམ་ཡང་འདིས་ཆོད་པ་ཡིན་ནོ༔ ལས་ཉོན་བག་ཆགས་ཀྱི་དྲི་མ་ཡང་འདིས་འདག་པ་ཡིན་ནོ༔ སྐུ་གསུམ་གྱི་ཞིང་ཁམས་ཀྱང་འདིས་འགྲོངས་པ་ཡིན་ནོ༔

རིགས་ཀྱི་བུ་དག་སྙན་གསོན་ཅིག༔
རྒྱལ་བ་ཀུན་གྱིས་བྱིན་བརླབས་པས༔
ཡང་སྙིང་འདུས་པའི་སྙིང་པོ་འདི༔
ཕན་བདེ་ཀུན་གྱི་འབྱུང་གནས་ཡིན༔
དངོས་གྲུབ་ཀུན་གྱི་རྩ་བ་ཡིན༔
མཐོ་རིས་བགྲོད་པའི་སྐས་ཀ་ཡིན༔
ངན་སོང་དགག་པའི་སྒོ་མོ་ཡིན༔
འཁོར་བ་སྒྲོལ་བའི་གྲུ་གཟིངས་ཡིན༔
མུན་པ་སེལ་བའི་སྒྲོན་མེ་ཡིན༔
དུག་ལྔ་འཇོམས་པའི་དཔའ་བོ་ཡིན༔
སྡིག་སྒྲིབ་བསྲེག་པའི་མེ་དཔུང་ཡིན༔
སྡུག་བསྔལ་བཏུང་བའི་ཐོ་བ་ཡིན༔
མཐའ་ཁོབ་འདུལ་བའི་གཉེན་པོ་ཡིན༔
ཁ་བ་ཅན་གྱི་ཆོས་སྐལ་ཡིན༔
མདོ་རྒྱུད་བསྟན་བཅོས་དུ་མ་དང༔

ཐོས་བསམ་སྒོམ་གསུམ་ཐམས་ཅད་ཀྱིཿ
སྙིང་པོ་གཅིག་ཏུ་བསྡུས་པའི་བཅུདཿ
གཅིག་ཆོག་རྒྱལ་པོ་རིན་པོ་ཆེཿ
ཡི་གེ་དྲུག་པ་འདི་བློས་ཤིགཿ

ཅེས་སོགས་བཀའ་གཏེར་ཐམས་ཅད་ནས་རྒྱ་ཆེར་འབྱུང་བ་བརྗོད་ཀྱིས་མི་ལངས་ཤིང་། གསུང་ཡི་གེ་དྲུག་པ་འདི་དད་པ་དང་ལྡན་པས་ལན་གཅིག་བརྗོད་ཀྱང་འདི་ལྟ་བུའི་ཕན་ཡོན་འབྱུང་ངེས་ཡིན་པས། སྒོ་གསུམ་ཐ་མལ་དུ་མ་བསྐྱུར་བར། ཚོགས་ཆུང་ལ་དོན་ཆེ་བའི་དགེ་ཚོགས་རླབས་པོ་ཆེ་འདི་ཉིད་ལ་ཉིན་རེར་ཁྲི་ནས་བརྒྱ་ཙ་ཡན་རྒྱུན་དུ་ཆགས་མེད་གཡར་དམ་དུ་བླངས་ནས་མི་ལུས་དོན་ལྡན་ཅེས་ཀྱང་མཛད་འཚལ་ལོ།།

འཕགས་པའི་ཐུགས་རྗེའི་དཔུངས་ཐག་གིས།
འགྲོ་བ་སྲིད་མཚོ་ལས་དྲངས་ཏེ།
རྣམ་གྲོལ་བདེ་ཆེན་ཐར་བའི་གླིང་།
རི་བོ་ཏ་ལར་དབུག་དབྱུང་གསོལ།

ཞེས་པའང་རིགས་ལྡན་ཆོས་མཛད་མ་སྐལ་བཟང་སྒྲོལ་དཀར་དང་། མ་ཡུམ་ཚེ་བརྟེན་སྒྲོལ་དཀར་ལགས་བཅས་ནས་འདི་ལྟར་སྦྱོར་ཞེས་བསྐུལ་ནས་དུས་རིང་མོར་འདས་ཤིང་སླར་ཡང་ནན་ཏན་གྱིས་བསྐྱར་བསྐུལ་ཡང་ཡང་བྱུང་བའི་གཡར་ཁྲལ་དུ་རང་འདྲའི་བློ་དམན་ཅན་གྱི་ཁྲིམ་པ་རྣན་པོས་གོ་བདེར་བྲིས་ཏེ། དུས་ངན་གྱི་བྱང་ཆུབ་སེམས་དཔའི་མིང་དུ་ཁས་འཆེ་བ། ཆོས་ལྟར་བཅོས་པའི་སྨྲ་ཧོ་བ་བློ་གྲོས་གཟི་བརྗིད་དམ། མིང་གཞན་མཁའ་ཁྱབ་རྡོ་རྗེར་འབོད་པའི་རྣན་པོ་ནད་བུ་ཅན་གྱི་སྨུག་ལས་སོ།། །།དགེ་ལེགས་འཕེལ།། །།

༄། བྱང་ཆུབ་སྤྱོད་ཚུལ་སྙིང་པོར་དྲིལ་བ་རྒྱལ་སྲས་ལག་
ལེན་སོ་བདུན་མ་ཞེས་བྱ་བ་བཞུགས་སོ།

THE TIBETAN TEXT:

The Thirty-Seven Practices of Bodhisattvas

by **Ngulchu Thogme**

༄༅། བྱང་ཆུབ་སྤྱོད་ཚུལ་སྙིང་པོར་དྲིལ་བ་རྒྱལ་སྲས་ལག་
ལེན་སོ་བདུན་མ་ཞེས་བྱ་བ་བཞུགས་སོ།

ན་མོ་ལོ་ཀེ་ཤྭ་ར་ཡ།།

གང་གིས་ཆོས་ཀུན་འགྲོ་འོང་མེད་གཟིགས་ཀྱང་།།
འགྲོ་བའི་དོན་ལ་གཅིག་ཏུ་བརྩོན་མཛད་པ།།
བླ་མ་མཆོག་དང་སྤྱན་རས་གཟིགས་མགོན་ལ།།
རྟག་ཏུ་སྒོ་གསུམ་གུས་པས་ཕྱག་འཚལ་ལོ།།

ཕན་བདེའི་འབྱུང་གནས་རྫོགས་པའི་སངས་རྒྱས་རྣམས།།
དམ་ཆོས་བསྒྲུབས་ལས་བྱུང་སྟེ་དེ་ཡང་ནི།།
དེ་ཡི་ལག་ལེན་ཤེས་ལ་རག་ལས་པས།།
རྒྱལ་སྲས་རྣམས་ཀྱི་ལག་ལེན་བཤད་པར་བྱ།།

དལ་འབྱོར་གྲུ་ཆེན་རྙེད་དཀའ་ཐོབ་དུས་འདིར།།
བདག་གཞན་འཁོར་བའི་མཚོ་ལས་བསྒྲལ་བྱའི་ཕྱིར།།
ཉིན་དང་མཚན་དུ་གཡེལ་བ་མེད་པར་ནི།།
ཉན་སེམས་བསྒོམ་པ་རྒྱལ་སྲས་ལག་ལེན་ཡིན།། ༡

གཉེན་གྱི་ཕྱོགས་ལ་འདོད་ཆགས་ཆུ་ལྟར་གཡོ།།
དགྲ་ཡི་ཕྱོགས་ལ་ཞེ་སྡང་མེ་ལྟར་འབར།།
བླང་དོར་བརྗེད་པའི་གཏི་མུག་མུན་ནག་ཅན།།
ཕ་ཡུལ་སྤོང་བ་རྒྱལ་སྲས་ལག་ལེན་ཡིན།། ༢

ཡུལ་ངན་སྤངས་པས་ཉོན་མོངས་རིམ་གྱིས་འགྲིབ།།
རྣམ་གཡེང་མེད་པས་དགེ་སྦྱོར་ངང་གིས་འཕེལ།།
རིག་པ་དྭངས་པས་ཆོས་ལ་ངེས་ཤེས་སྐྱེ།།
དབེན་པ་བསྟེན་པ་རྒྱལ་སྲས་ལག་ལེན་ཡིན།། ༣

ཡུན་རིང་འགྲོགས་པའི་མཛའ་བཤེས་སོ་སོར་འབྲལ།།
འབད་པས་བསྒྲུགས་པའི་ནོར་རྫས་ཤུལ་དུ་ལུས།།
ལུས་ཀྱི་མགྲོན་ཁང་རྣམ་ཤེས་མགྲོན་པོས་བོར།།
ཚེ་འདི་བློས་གཏོང་རྒྱལ་སྲས་ལག་ལེན་ཡིན།། ༤

གང་དང་འགྲོགས་ན་དུག་གསུམ་འཕེལ་འགྱུར་ཞིང་།།
ཐོས་བསམ་སྒོམ་པའི་བྱ་བ་ཉམས་འགྱུར་བ།།
བྱམས་དང་སྙིང་རྗེ་མེད་པར་བསྒྱུར་བྱེད་པའི།།
གྲོགས་ངན་སྤོང་བ་རྒྱལ་སྲས་ལག་ལེན་ཡིན།། ༥

གང་ཞིག་བསྟེན་ན་ཉེས་པ་ཟད་འགྱུར་ཞིང་།།
ཡོན་ཏན་ཡར་ངོའི་ཟླ་ལྟར་འཕེལ་འགྱུར་བའི།།
བཤེས་གཉེན་དམ་པ་རང་གི་ལུས་བས་ཀྱང་།།
གཅེས་པར་འཛིན་པ་རྒྱལ་སྲས་ལག་ལེན་ཡིན།། ༦

རང་ཡང་འཁོར་བའི་བཙོན་རར་བཅིངས་པ་ཡི།།
འཇིག་རྟེན་ལྷ་ཡིས་སུ་ཞིག་སྐྱོབ་པར་ནུས།།
དེ་ཕྱིར་གང་ལ་སྐྱབས་ན་མི་བསླུ་བའི།།
དཀོན་མཆོག་སྐྱབས་འགྲོ་རྒྱལ་སྲས་ལག་ལེན་ཡིན།། ༧

ཤིན་ཏུ་བཟོད་དཀའི་ངན་སོང་སྡུག་བསྔལ་རྣམས།།
སྡིག་པའི་ལས་ཀྱི་འབྲས་བུར་ཐུབ་པས་གསུངས།།
དེ་ཕྱིར་སྲོག་ལ་བབ་ཀྱང་སྡིག་པའི་ལས།།
ནམ་ཡང་མི་བྱེད་རྒྱལ་སྲས་ལག་ལེན་ཡིན།། ༨

སྲིད་གསུམ་བདེ་བ་རྩྭ་རྩེའི་ཟིལ་པ་བཞིན།།
ཡུད་ཙམ་ཞིག་གིས་འཇིག་པའི་ཆོས་ཅན་ཡིན།།
ནམ་ཡང་མི་འགྱུར་ཐར་པའི་གོ་འཕང་མཆོག །
དོན་དུ་གཉེར་བ་རྒྱལ་སྲས་ལག་ལེན་ཡིན།། ༩

ཐོག་མེད་དུས་ནས་བདག་ལ་བརྩེ་བ་ཅན།།
མ་རྣམས་སྡུག་ན་རང་བདེས་ཅི་ཞིག་བྱ།།
དེ་ཕྱིར་མཐའ་ཡས་སེམས་ཅན་བསྒྲལ་བྱའི་ཕྱིར།།
བྱང་ཆུབ་སེམས་བསྐྱེད་རྒྱལ་སྲས་ལག་ལེན་ཡིན།། ༡༠

སྡུག་བསྔལ་མ་ལུས་བདག་བདེ་འདོད་ལས་བྱུང་།།
རྫོགས་པའི་སངས་རྒྱས་གཞན་ཕན་སེམས་ལས་འཁྲུངས།།
དེ་ཕྱིར་བདག་བདེ་གཞན་གྱི་སྡུག་བསྔལ་དག །
ཡང་དག་བརྗེ་བ་རྒྱལ་སྲས་ལག་ལེན་ཡིན།། ༡༡

སུ་དག་འདོད་ཆེན་དབང་གིས་བདག་གི་ནོར།།
ཐམས་ཅད་འཕྲོག་གམ་འཕྲོག་ཏུ་འཇུག་ན་ཡང་།།
ལུས་དང་ལོངས་སྤྱོད་དུས་གསུམ་དགེ་བ་རྣམས།།
དེ་ལ་བསྔོ་བ་རྒྱལ་སྲས་ལག་ལེན་ཡིན།། ༡༢

བདག་ལ་ཉེས་པ་ཅུང་ཟད་མེད་བཞིན་དུ།།
གཞན་དག་བདག་གི་མགོ་བོ་གཅོད་བྱེད་ནའང་།།
སྙིང་རྗེའི་དབང་གིས་དེ་ཡི་སྡིག་པ་རྣམས།།
བདག་ལ་ལེན་པ་རྒྱལ་སྲས་ལག་ལེན་ཡིན།། ༡༣

འགའ་ཞིག་བདག་ལ་མི་སྙན་སྣ་ཚོགས་པ།།
སྟོང་གསུམ་ཁྱབ་པར་སྒྲོགས་པར་བྱེད་ན་ཡང་།།
བྱམས་པའི་སེམས་ཀྱིས་སླར་ཡང་དེ་ཉིད་ཀྱི།།
ཡོན་ཏན་བརྗོད་པ་རྒྱལ་སྲས་ལག་ལེན་ཡིན།། ༡༤

འགྲོ་མང་འདུས་པའི་དབུས་སུ་འགའ་ཞིག་གིས།།
མཚང་ནས་བྲུས་ཤིང་ཚིག་ངན་སྨྲ་ན་ཡང་།།
དེ་ལ་དགེ་བའི་བཤེས་ཀྱི་འདུ་ཤེས་ཀྱིས།།
གུས་པར་འདུད་པ་རྒྱལ་སྲས་ལག་ལེན་ཡིན།། ༡༥

བདག་གི་བུ་བཞིན་གཅེས་པར་བསྐྱངས་པའི་མིས།།
བདག་ལ་དགྲ་བཞིན་བལྟ་བར་བྱེད་ན་ཡང་།།
ནད་ཀྱིས་བཏབ་པའི་བུ་ལ་མ་བཞིན་དུ།།
ལྷག་པར་བརྩེ་བ་རྒྱལ་སྲས་ལག་ལེན་ཡིན།། ༡༦

རང་དང་མཉམ་པའམ་དམན་པའི་སྐྱེ་བོ་ཡིས།།
ང་རྒྱལ་དབང་གིས་བརྙས་ཐབས་བྱེད་ན་ཡང་།།
བླ་མ་བཞིན་དུ་གུས་པས་བདག་ཉིད་ཀྱི།།
སྤྱི་བོར་ལེན་པ་རྒྱལ་སྲས་ལག་ལེན་ཡིན།། ༡༧

འཚོ་བས་ཕོངས་ཤིང་རྟག་ཏུ་མི་ཡིས་བརྙས།།
ཚབས་ཆེན་ནད་དང་གདོན་གྱིས་བཏབ་ཀྱང་སླར།།
འགྲོ་ཀུན་སྡིག་སྡུག་བདག་ལ་ལེན་བྱེད་ཅིང་།།
ཞུམ་པ་མེད་པ་རྒྱལ་སྲས་ལག་ལེན་ཡིན།། ༡༨

སྙན་པར་གྲགས་ཤིང་འགྲོ་མང་སྤྱི་བོས་བཏུད།།
རྣམ་ཐོས་བུ་ཡི་ནོར་འདྲ་ཐོབ་གྱུར་ཀྱང་།།
སྲིད་པའི་དཔལ་འབྱོར་སྙིང་པོ་མེད་གཟིགས་ནས།།
ཁེངས་པ་མེད་པ་རྒྱལ་སྲས་ལག་ལེན་ཡིན།། ༡༩

རང་གི་ཞེ་སྡང་དགྲ་བོ་མ་ཐུལ་ན།།
ཕྱི་རོལ་དགྲ་བོ་བཏུལ་ཞིང་འཕེལ་བར་འགྱུར།།
དེ་ཕྱིར་བྱམས་དང་སྙིང་རྗེའི་དམག་དཔུང་གིས།།
རང་རྒྱུད་འདུལ་བ་རྒྱལ་སྲས་ལག་ལེན་ཡིན།། ༢༠

འདོད་པའི་ཡོན་ཏན་ལན་ཚྭའི་ཆུ་དང་འདྲ།།
ཇི་ཙམ་སྤྱད་ཀྱང་སྲེད་པ་འཕེལ་བར་འགྱུར།།
གང་ལ་ཞེན་ཆགས་སྐྱེ་བའི་དངོས་པོ་རྣམས།།
འཕྲལ་ལ་སྤོང་བ་རྒྱལ་སྲས་ལག་ལེན་ཡིན།། ༢༡

ཇི་ལྟར་སྣང་བ་འདི་དག་རང་གི་སེམས།།
སེམས་ཉིད་གདོད་ནས་སྤྲོས་པའི་མཐའ་དང་བྲལ།།
དེ་ཉིད་ཤེས་ནས་གཟུང་འཛིན་མཚན་མ་རྣམས།།
ཡིད་ལ་མི་བྱེད་རྒྱལ་སྲས་ལག་ལེན་ཡིན།། ༢༢

ཡིད་དུ་འོང་བའི་ཡུལ་དང་འཕྲད་པ་ན།།
དབྱར་གྱི་དུས་ཀྱི་འཇའ་ཚོན་ཇི་བཞིན་དུ།།
མཛེས་པར་སྣང་ཡང་བདེན་པར་མི་ལྟ་ཞིང་།།
ཞེན་ཆགས་སྤོང་བ་རྒྱལ་སྲས་ལག་ལེན་ཡིན།། ༢༣

སྡུག་བསྔལ་སྣ་ཚོགས་རྨི་ལམ་བུ་ཤི་ལྟར།།
འཁྲུལ་སྣང་བདེན་པར་བཟུང་བས་ཨ་ཐང་ཆད།།
དེ་ཕྱིར་མི་མཐུན་རྐྱེན་དང་འཕྲད་པའི་ཚེ།།
འཁྲུལ་པར་ལྟ་བ་རྒྱལ་སྲས་ལག་ལེན་ཡིན།། ༢༤

བྱང་ཆུབ་འདོད་པས་ལུས་ཀྱང་གཏོང་དགོས་ན།།
ཕྱི་རོལ་དངོས་པོ་རྣམས་ལ་སྨོས་ཅི་དགོས།།
དེ་ཕྱིར་ལན་དང་རྣམ་སྨིན་མི་རེ་བའི།།
སྦྱིན་པ་གཏོང་བ་རྒྱལ་སྲས་ལག་ལེན་ཡིན།། ༢༥

ཚུལ་ཁྲིམས་མེད་པར་རང་དོན་མི་འགྲུབ་ན།།
གཞན་དོན་སྒྲུབ་པར་འདོད་པ་གད་མོའི་གནས།།
དེ་ཕྱིར་སྲིད་པའི་འདུན་པ་མེད་པ་ཡི།།
ཚུལ་ཁྲིམས་སྲུང་བ་རྒྱལ་སྲས་ལག་ལེན་ཡིན།། ༢༦

དགེ་བའི་ལོངས་སྤྱོད་འདོད་པའི་རྒྱལ་སྲས་ལ།།
གནོད་བྱེད་ཐམས་ཅད་རིན་ཆེན་གཏེར་དང་མཚུངས།།
དེ་ཕྱིར་ཀུན་ལ་ཞེ་འགྲས་མེད་པ་ཡི།།
བཟོད་པ་སྒོམ་པ་རྒྱལ་སྲས་ལག་ལེན་ཡིན།། ༢༧

རང་དོན་འབའ་ཞིག་སྒྲུབ་པའི་ཉན་རང་ཡང་།།
མགོ་ལ་མེ་ཤོར་བཟློག་ལྟར་བརྩོན་མཐོང་ན།།
འགྲོ་ཀུན་དོན་དུ་ཡོན་ཏན་འབྱུང་གནས་ཀྱི།།
བརྩོན་འགྲུས་རྩོམ་པ་རྒྱལ་སྲས་ལག་ལེན་ཡིན།། ༢༨

ཞི་གནས་རབ་ཏུ་ལྡན་པའི་ལྷག་མཐོང་གིས།།
ཉོན་མོངས་རྣམ་པར་འཇོམས་པར་ཤེས་བྱས་ནས།།
གཟུགས་མེད་བཞི་ལས་ཡང་དག་འདས་པ་ཡི།།
བསམ་གཏན་སྒོམ་པ་རྒྱལ་སྲས་ལག་ལེན་ཡིན།། ༢༩

ཤེས་རབ་མེད་ན་ཕ་རོལ་ཕྱིན་ལྔ་ཡིས།།
རྫོགས་པའི་བྱང་ཆུབ་ཐོབ་པར་མི་ནུས་པས།།
ཐབས་དང་ལྡན་ཞིང་འཁོར་གསུམ་མི་རྟོག་པའི།།
ཤེས་རབ་སྒོམ་པ་རྒྱལ་སྲས་ལག་ལེན་ཡིན།། ༣༠

རང་གི་འཁྲུལ་པ་རང་གིས་མ་བརྟགས་ན།།
ཆོས་པའི་གཟུགས་ཀྱིས་ཆོས་མིན་བྱེད་སྲིད་པས།།
དེ་ཕྱིར་རྒྱུན་དུ་རང་གི་འཁྲུལ་པ་ལ།།
བརྟགས་ནས་སྤོང་བ་རྒྱལ་སྲས་ལག་ལེན་ཡིན།། ༣༡

ཉོན་མོངས་དབང་གིས་རྒྱལ་སྲས་གཞན་དག་གི །
ཉེས་པ་གླེང་ན་བདག་ཉིད་ཉམས་འགྱུར་བས།།
ཐེག་པ་ཆེ་ལ་ཞུགས་པའི་གང་ཟག་གི །
ཉེས་པ་མི་སྨྲ་རྒྱལ་སྲས་ལག་ལེན་ཡིན།། ༣༢

རྙེད་བཀུར་དབང་གིས་ཕན་ཚུན་རྩོད་འགྱུར་ཞིང་།།
ཐོས་བསམ་སྒོམ་པའི་བྱ་བ་ཉམས་འགྱུར་བས།།
མཛའ་བཤེས་ཁྱིམ་དང་སྦྱིན་བདག་ཁྱིམ་རྣམས་ལ།།
ཆགས་པ་སྤོང་བ་རྒྱལ་སྲས་ལག་ལེན་ཡིན།། ༣༣

རྩུབ་མོའི་ཚིག་གིས་གཞན་སེམས་འཁྲུག་འགྱུར་ཞིང་།།
རྒྱལ་བའི་སྲས་ཀྱི་སྤྱོད་ཚུལ་ཉམས་འགྱུར་བས།།
དེ་ཕྱིར་གཞན་གྱི་ཡིད་དུ་མི་འོང་བའི།།
ཚིག་རྩུབ་སྤོང་བ་རྒྱལ་སྲས་ལག་ལེན་ཡིན།། ༣༤

ཉོན་མོངས་གོམས་ན་གཉེན་པོས་བཟློག་དཀའ་བས།།
དྲན་ཤེས་སྐྱེས་བུས་གཉེན་པོའི་མཚོན་བཟུང་ནས།།
ཆགས་སོགས་ཉོན་མོངས་དང་པོ་སྐྱེས་མ་ཐག །
འབུར་འཇོམས་བྱེད་པ་རྒྱལ་སྲས་ལག་ལེན་ཡིན།། ༣༥

མདོར་ན་གང་དུ་སྤྱོད་ལམ་ཅི་བྱེད་ཀྱང་།།
རང་གི་སེམས་ཀྱི་གནས་སྐབས་ཅི་འདྲ་ཞེས།།
རྒྱུན་དུ་དྲན་དང་ཤེས་བཞིན་ལྡན་པ་ཡིས།།
གཞན་དོན་སྒྲུབ་པ་རྒྱལ་སྲས་ལག་ལེན་ཡིན།། ༣༦

དེ་ལྟར་བརྩོན་པས་བསྒྲུབས་པའི་དགེ་བ་རྣམས༎
མཐའ་ཡས་འགྲོ་བའི་སྡུག་བསྔལ་བསལ་བའི་ཕྱིར༎
འཁོར་གསུམ་རྣམ་པར་དག་པའི་ཤེས་རབ་ཀྱིས༎
བྱང་ཆུབ་བསྔོ་བ་རྒྱལ་སྲས་ལག་ལེན་ཡིན༎ ༣༧

མདོ་དང་བསྟན་བཅོས་རྣམས་ལས་གསུངས་པའི་དོན༎
དམ་པ་རྣམས་ཀྱི་གསུང་གི་རྗེས་འབྲང་ནས༎
རྒྱལ་སྲས་རྣམས་ཀྱི་ལག་ལེན་སུམ་བཅུ་བདུན༎
རྒྱལ་སྲས་ལམ་ལ་སློབ་འདོད་དོན་དུ་བཀོད༎

བློ་གྲོས་དམན་ཞིང་སྦྱང་པ་ཆུང་བའི་ཕྱིར༎
མཁས་པ་དགྱེས་པའི་སྡེབ་སྦྱོར་མ་མཆིས་ཏེ༎
མདོ་དང་དམ་པའི་གསུང་ལ་བརྟེན་པའི་ཕྱིར༎
རྒྱལ་སྲས་ལག་ལེན་འཁྲུལ་མེད་ལགས་པར་སེམས༎

འོན་ཀྱང་རྒྱལ་སྲས་སྤྱོད་པ་རླབས་ཆེན་རྣམས༎
བློ་དམན་བདག་འདྲས་གཏིང་དཔག་དཀའ་བའི་ཕྱིར༎
འགལ་དང་མ་འབྲེལ་ལ་སོགས་ཉེས་པའི་ཚོགས༎
དམ་པ་རྣམས་ཀྱིས་བཟོད་པར་མཛད་དུ་གསོལ༎

དེ་ལས་བྱུང་བའི་དགེ་བས་འགྲོ་བ་ཀུན༎
དོན་དམ་ཀུན་རྫོབ་བྱང་ཆུབ་སེམས་མཆོག་གིས༎
སྲིད་དང་ཞི་བའི་མཐའ་ལ་མི་གནས་པའི༎
སྤྱན་རས་གཟིགས་མགོན་དེ་དང་མཚུངས་པར་ཤོག །

ཅེས་པ་འདི་རང་གཞན་ལ་ཕན་པའི་དོན་དུ་ལུང་དང་རིགས་པ་སྨྲ་བའི་
བཙུན་པ་ཐོགས་མེད་ཀྱིས་དངུལ་ཆུའི་རིན་ཆེན་ཕུག་ཏུ་སྦྱར་བའོ། ༎

ॐ मणि पद्मे हूँ

List of Illustrations